GETTING AN
ACADEMIC JOB

SURVIVAL SKILLS FOR SCHOLARS

Managing Editor: Peter Labella

Survival Skills for Scholars provides you, the professor or advanced graduate student working in a college or university setting, with practical suggestions for making the most of your academic career. These brief, readable guides will help you with skills that you are required to master as a college professor but may have never been taught in graduate school. Using hands-on, jargon-free advice and examples, forms, lists, and suggestions for additional resources, experts on different aspects of academic life give invaluable tips on managing the day-to-day tasks of academia—effectively and efficiently.

Volumes in This Series

SURVIVAL SKILLS FOR SCHOLARS

GETTING AN ACADEMIC JOB

JENNIE JACOBS KRONENFELD
MARCIA LYNN WHICKER

SAGE Publications
International Educational and Professional Publisher
Thousand Oaks   London   New Delhi

For information address:

SAGE Publications, Inc.
2455 Teller Road
Newbury Park, California 91320
E-mail: order@sagepub.com

SAGE Publications Ltd.
6 Bonhill Street
London EC2A 4PU
United Kingdom

SAGE Publications India Pvt. Ltd.
M-32 Market
Greater Kailash I
New Delhi 110 048 India

Printed in the United States of America

Library of Congress Cataloging-in-Publication Data

Kronenfeld, Jennie J.
    Getting an academic job: strategies for success / authors,
Jennie Jacobs Kronenfeld and Marcia Lynn Whicker.
        p. cm.—(Survival skills for scholars; v. 17)
    Includes bibliographical references.
    ISBN 0-8039-7015-3 (pbk.: acid-free paper).—ISBN 0-8039-7014-5
(cloth: acid-free paper)
    1. College teachers—Employment—United States. 2. Graduate
students—Employment—United States. 3. Job hunting—United States.
I. Whicker, Marcia Lynn. II. Title. III. Series.

LB2332.72.K76 1997   96-25375

97 98 99 00 01 02 03 10 9 8 7 6 5 4 3 2 1

Acquiring Editor:	Peter Labella
Editorial Assistant:	Frances Borghi
Production Editor:	Sherrise Purdum
Production Assistant:	Karen Wiley
Typesetter/Designer:	Marion Warren
Cover Designer:	Lesa Valdez

Contents

1 | The Nature of Job Searches

This book will describe the process of how you find an academic job. Your success depends on how many job candidates are looking at the same time as you are and how many and what type of employers need new PhDs—factors you cannot control. But it also depends on your own training, capabilities, skills, recommendations, and presentation of self—aspects of your search more readily within your control. We will discuss here the factors that may facilitate and impede your search. We will particularly focus on those factors that you can control, so that you will be among those who succeed in finding an employer.

A Tale of Two Job Candidates

Consider the case of two job candidates, Paul and Mary. Both began their job search in the same year. Both had worked hard in graduate school and felt they could make meaningful contributions to their fields. Each looked forward to the initial job and the end of the graduate school grind.

Paul was in history and Mary was in economics. Paul was eager to write the definitive work on 19th-century America. Mary wished to expand the framework of neoclassical economics beyond questions of production to include questions of distribution.

Both Paul and Mary had gained some exposure to teaching at the college level while still graduate students and looked forward to developing their teaching skills. They expressed enthusiasm for stimulating students with ideas and Socratic questioning. Each wished to imbue students with his or her own newly polished skills of critical thinking. Each anticipated giving students ample attention through generous office hours, becoming advisers to those undergraduates most interested in their respective fields, and providing opportunities for students to write probing papers on significant topics. Both Paul and Mary were working on their dissertations and had made substantial progress as the time for job searches began. Paul chose to study the impact of American myths on the cultural, social, and political fabric of the United States in the 1800s. Mary's dissertation topic was the equity and efficiency impacts of industrial regulations on the U.S. and British economies.

But despite these similarities, Paul and Mary differed in their approaches to finding the first academic job. Paul's approach was unorganized and at times even indifferent. He apparently assumed that his previous academic success would continue into his academic career without planning and effort.

Paul had always been a successful student and, indeed, a success at most things in life. He had attended an excellent high school in the Midwest and a small high-caliber liberal arts college in the Northeast, funded by his parents. He had remained in the Northeast for graduate school, selecting a well-regarded state university where he was offered a competitive university fellowship for his first two years of graduate study. Subsequently, he obtained teaching assistantships to complete his coursework.

Paul's adviser had encouraged him to apply for a dissertation grant to support his research, and he did so. When his dissertation was not fully completed after the grant ran out, his doctoral department patched together some adjunct teaching, both at his own PhD university and through contacts at a nearby college, to sustain him while he continued writing his dissertation. After two years of these ad hoc arrangements, however, Paul's adviser urged him strongly to go on the job market and search for a "real" job. By this time, seven years had elapsed from the time Paul entered graduate school, and the adviser felt that Paul should now embark on his career.

Paul was somewhat conflicted about his impending foray into the job market, although he could not articulate those emotions to himself, much less to his adviser. Paul enjoyed the big-city atmosphere and cultural amenities of the urban area in which his doctoral university was located in contrast to the middle-class, middle-America, midwestern town in which he had been raised. He was also involved in a relationship with a fellow graduate student in comparative literature. They had not had a serious discussion about finding jobs nor about the future of their relationship.

As with many naive students, Paul's first hope was that a wonderful job in the same urban area would miraculously appear. Only when his adviser urged him, did he apply for jobs outside the Northeast. Reflecting his ambivalence, Paul seized on the slightest imperfection in prospective jobs and employers to either not apply or downplay their advantages. As the year progressed, Paul applied mostly to universities as prestigious (or slightly less so) as his doctoral institution and to elite small liberal arts colleges. Only with urging would he apply to an occasional four-year state college or less prestigious university.

The job applications and letters took time. The emotional strain of searching took energy away from completing his dissertation. His progress on it slowed and his projected completion expanded to a more distant and not well-defined date.

Paul interviewed at the national history meetings in mid-winter with representatives from two colleges and a university. One was, in his assessment, a mediocre state university in a distant state in the South, to which he had little interest in moving. A second conference interview was with a representative from a small liberal arts college in the Midwest, where teaching loads were quite high. A third interview was with a faculty member from an elite private college in the Northeast not too far from his PhD university. Paul was most excited about this interview.

By March, when he had no campus job interviews lined up, his spirits flagged and he became depressed. In early April, however, the elite private college called and invited him to a campus interview for a tenure-track job. The campus interview did not go as smoothly as he had hoped. Of the six faculty in the history department, one was away on personal business. Three had earned their PhDs at schools more prestigious than Paul's PhD university and during his interview talked critically about schools of "lower caliber" than those they had attended. The department chair seemed distracted by the administrative details of a national symposium the department was sponsoring in a month. One of the junior faculty seemed threatened by him and the possibility of competing with him to teach the 19th-century American history courses and for travel money.

As part of the interview process, Paul was asked both to teach an undergraduate class and make a research presentation on his dissertation to the faculty. The undergraduates challenged him more than those he had previously taught, asking for further proof and questioning his assumptions and biases. At the research presentation, one senior faculty member questioned the usefulness of his whole line of inquiry.

Although the campus interview did not go as well as Paul had hoped, he did not think he had blown his chances completely. But when he returned, days and then weeks went by with no contact from the college where he had interviewed, other than a reimbursement check for his expenses. At one point, he called the department but spoke only with the department secretary who said that the chair was out of town.

Finally, after two months, well into the summer and past the height of the job season, Paul received a letter from the department chair, thanking him for his interest in the job but stating that the position was now filled with a candidate who best met department needs. The rejection letter was professional—it wished him well on future endeavors but gave no clue as to why he had not been selected.

In contrast to Paul, who had made some key decisions on the basis of emotion without thinking through consequences, Mary approached her career realistically and methodically. She had grown up in the South and attended the major state university in her home state. Her father had not attended college but worked at a blue-collar job that eventually allowed him to rise into first-line supervisory skills. Her mother attended college for two years and worked in a local department store. Despite a modest upbringing, Mary was highly motivated and achievement oriented. She performed well in high school and in college, acquiring good grades and scholarships. In college, her fascination for the theoretical, along with her awareness of the importance of money, led her to study economics, undeterred that women students in her major were in the minority or that there were no women economics professors at her university. Nonetheless, she developed friendly relations with two of her major professors, who advised her to go to the best possible graduate school. Mary applied to graduate schools of high reputation and decided to attend a Big Ten university where she received financial aid.

Early in her graduate school experience, Mary carefully mapped out the subfields in which she wished to specialize. She also thought about which professors she wanted to work with. She decided to add one subfield that was particularly popular at the time, game theory, to increase her marketability. During graduate study, Mary tried to develop several seminar papers into publishable articles. She would approach professors with the idea of collaborating on a paper if it proved sufficiently interesting. By her last year of graduate school, she had had two papers accepted by regional journals and a third was in the process of being reviewed.

Because of her seriousness about publishing, Mary's professors knew her better than most of the other graduate students and wrote glowing letters of reference for her. As her year for job searching approached, her main adviser and another professor called up colleagues to put in a good word for her. Mary carefully scanned the professional publication that contained job announcements and identified a range of jobs, which she placed into three categories: Tier 1 was for jobs at places equivalent to her PhD university and even one or two better, where the competition would be very high and the probability of getting a job not so great as elsewhere. Tier 2 was for mostly state universities with some type of graduate program, but not always a PhD program. Tier 3 was for liberal arts colleges ranging from very good to just OK. Mary did not restrict her search to any part of the United States.

As is critical in the discipline of economics, Mary attended the national meetings in December for interviews. She also attended a regional meeting and delivered a conference paper there. She interviewed with nine different university representatives and returned home exhausted but glad she had completed initial interviews.

By early spring, Mary had received invitations for four campus interviews. One was a Tier 3 place, a liberal arts college. The second was a state university with an MA program in economics. The third was a major research university of similar quality to her graduate school institution, and the fourth was another four-year college.

Before Mary's first interview, her adviser arranged for her to practice, by giving a research colloquium on her dissertation topic to her fellow graduate students and professors. Her professors asked hard and penetrating questions, to prepare her for similar questions on interviews.

After the first two campus interviews, the four-year college called with an offer. Mary preferred to be at a research university; indeed, her third interview was to be at such a university in a nearby state. Mary was able to secure three weeks before having to respond to the college offer, and she went on the third interview. She liked the research university and found out that she was the last candidate on the interview list. She indicated while there that she had had an outstanding offer from another institution and would need a decision as early as possible.

Two days before her time to respond to the four-year college ran out, the university called with an offer that did not include quite as much money as the first, but she liked the location of the university and the opportunity to work with graduate students. After weighing the pros and cons of her two offers, she accepted the job at the research university.

Factors That Affect Your Job Search

The cases of Paul and Mary show that several factors influence the success of candidates in search of academic jobs. These factors operate at different levels but all influence whether a candidate will find a job and what type of job it will be. The rest of this chapter reviews seven different factors: demographics, the general academic job market, cultural diversity, conditions within the discipline, institution-specific issues, politics at one's current institution, and your personal background and assets.

Demographic Trends. Underlying the demand for education at all levels are demographic trends. The largest demographic trend in the post-World War II United States has been the baby boom. After World War II, beginning in 1946, the birthrate increased as people who had postponed beginning families due to the war and the economic uncertainty of the war began to marry and have children. Millions of additional children poured into the educational pipeline between the years of 1946 and 1964, when the baby boom era gave way to the baby bust era.

This population surge applied pressure to educational institutions throughout the entire pipeline, including higher education institutions at the pipeline's end. By the early 1960s, the beginning wave of baby boomers was approaching college, causing colleges to expand rapidly and the number of faculty positions to grow. Faculty mobility was high, and tenure in most colleges and universities was fairly easy to obtain, with lower publication requirements than is now the case.

By the mid-1970s, the baby boom-induced expansion was over for most colleges. Enrollments grew less rapidly and even declined in some institutions. This trend had, in turn, an impact on the number of faculty positions. With less expansion and a large number of faculty already tenured, tenure-track jobs became harder to find for new job market entrants. Mobility for faculty already employed also diminished, further reducing the number of positions opening up from turnover. By the 1980s, some of the children of baby boomers, the baby boomlet generation, were beginning to enter college, but the surge was less than might have been expected due to patterns of delayed childbearing by many boomers. Some colleges and universities recruited nontraditional older students to maintain or even expand enrollments.

To date, nothing equivalent to the huge expansion in higher education fueled, in part, by the pressure from the baby boom has occurred since the 1960s. The baby boom was expected to continue to have an indirect impact on academic job prospects for newly minted PhDs, in that the trends it set in motion were expected to disappear in the 1990s. In particular, the large number of faculty hired in the 1960s to accommodate baby boomers was expected to retire, creating new openings and opportunities for new PhDs to gain academic jobs. But two factors have undercut this anticipated surge (Magner, 1994). First, retirement laws were changed to eliminate mandatory retirement for faculty so that some chose not to retire as anticipated. Second, when some faculty did retire, hard-pressed university administrators often chose not to fill the vacancies but, rather, to use the reduced number of faculty to recoup costs.

The State of the General Academic Job Market. In addition to demographic trends, the general academic job market is affected by the state of the economy and the prevailing political climate. The state of the economy is particularly relevant to state universities and colleges, because economic conditions directly affect state revenue projections which, in turn, affect state budgets and allocations for higher education. As the economy improves and revenues are plentiful, funding for higher education often increases as well, resulting, in some instances, in new faculty positions being created and vacancies being filled. If the economy is stagnant, budgets do not increase as rapidly or may even be cut. Allocations for higher education may be cut and faculty positions may not be funded.

But the economy also affects the academic job market at both public and private universities by affecting federal funding for student assistance and the ability of parents and students to pay tuition. When the economy is booming, students and their families have greater capacities to pay college tuition costs. When it is stagnant, students may have greater difficulty and be forced to postpone college or go part-time. Ironically, harsh economic conditions may increase graduate school enrollments as students, unable to find jobs with an undergraduate degree, decide to go to graduate school to become more competitive. These decisions of individuals, multiplied by millions, affect the demand for university and college faculty.

In addition to the economy, in a particular state the political climate may be either supportive or unsupportive of higher education. Again, the impact is particularly great on state-funded colleges and universities. In states that are supportive, the economic future of the state may be viewed as tied to the overall education level of its citizens and to creating an atmosphere favorable to research. In states that are less supportive, education may not be viewed as closely linked to economic development. Even if education dollars are available, a political battle may occur for those dollars between K through 12 schools on the one hand and higher education on the other. The outcome of the battle affects the funding for faculty positions.

One negative influence of the state on the general academic job market is a growing questioning of the value of higher education (and perhaps especially graduate education) by many state legislatures (Mahtesian, 1995). Some states are not increasing university budgets, even when their own economies are doing well. Others are mandating critical examinations of workload policies and tenure, which may have an impact on the most basic ways in which universities have operated in the United States since the end of World War II. Some states may dictate higher teaching loads, others may revise tenure. All of this questioning of the role of higher education in states may limit any future growth or vitality in publicly funded higher education.

The Need for Cultural Diversity. Most colleges and universities have been under some pressure to become more representative of the students they serve and of the overall population, beginning with the student debates and growth of affirmative action programs in the late 1960s and early 1970s. The pressure, again, may be greater at state colleges and universities, but due to federal funding constraints, all universities accepting federal research monies and financial assistance for students have needed to demonstrate ongoing efforts to ensure cultural diversity among the faculty. This whole situation is now undergoing rapid change. A recent court decision in Texas has removed affirmative action requirements in admissions to programs in Texas. The Regents of the University of California system are also eliminating affirmative action in admissions to programs. Thus, by the mid- to late 1990s, the role of affirmative action and cultural diversity among faculty is less clear than in 1990. Although most university administrators say that a more diversified faculty will remain a goal whether or not mandated by state or federal laws, the extent to which these policies may actually change is not clear at this point.

For the last twenty years, advertisements for academic jobs have generally carried a stock phrase about the institution's being an equal opportunity employer and that minorities and women are especially encouraged to apply. The implication has been that job candidates from population pools previously underrepresented in academia will have higher probabilities of getting a job than will white males. Despite these assertions, minorities and women remain underrepresented in most academic disciplines. Little systematic evidence exists that minorities and women have significantly higher prospects of employment than do white males. Changing requirements in affirmative action may alter the way targeted hires and special positions have been created. Some institutions, however, will continue to respond to student pressure by expanding their faculty diversity.

Demand for and Conditions Within Your Discipline. As the cases of Paul and Mary illustrate, some academic disciplines have a greater demand for faculty than do others. In part, the demand is a function of the number of candidates. Some fields, particularly in liberal arts and humanities, may have more candidates than others. But even in areas such as the sciences where there may be shortages, the current job market is fairly tight. In the last two years, articles about the lack of tenure-track positions have been published in newsletters and newspapers. The number of actual tenure-track openings is down in most disciplines. In general, in those fields where PhDs can be employed outside of academics as well as within it, the prospects of finding an appropriate job (even if not in the academy in a tenure-track line) are greater. Employment elsewhere, in research organizations, corporations, and government provides a safety valve to prevent the pools of unemployed PhDs searching for academic jobs from building up as large as they otherwise would. In Paul's case, historians with PhDs have fewer opportunities for employment outside teaching than do economists, the field in which Mary was earning her PhD.

Institutional Constraints and Politics at the Institution Where You Are Interviewing. Institutions where you might interview have constraints, particularly financial ones. Some institutions may be unsure at the start of the academic job market season whether or not funding for a position will, in fact, materialize. But the lead time needed to put together a job description is long. It involves departmental discussions about what subfields are needed and some attempt to reach consensus on the character of the position. It also involves contacting various discipline publications and outlets for publicizing jobs and leaving sufficient time for interested candidates to respond. In addition, going through the various vitae; making a decision, often by committee, about whom to interview; arranging the campus interviews and having the finalists come to the campus; and then reaching a decision also take time.

Some departments may go ahead and begin the search without any certainty that funding for the position will be there, stating in their advertisement that the position will be filled depending on funding availability. Such departments fear that if they wait until the funding is certain, the season will be too advanced and the best job candidates will already have taken jobs elsewhere. Institutional politics at prospective employer institutions, then, may affect position funding and your prospects for getting a job. Sometimes you may apply for a position and then not hear for a long time what has happened. You may conclude that the department was not interested in you when, in reality, funding for the position was withdrawn or never materialized as anticipated.

Institutional politics in departments where you are seeking a job also affect the decision about who will finally be hired. In theory, employing institutions want the best possible candidate, but the reality is that each faculty member in the hiring department has his or her own personal agenda. Some may have personal agendas not that different from the preceding objective, but others may put personal interest above department interests and fear a candidate who they believe will perform better than the norm. Although highly successful faculty will not be readily threatened by capable candidates, less successful faculty may be. But even beyond that, sincere differences about department needs may result in different views of which candidates are preferred and could contribute the most to the department. The politics in departments where you are seeking employment, then, affects how you will be viewed and the likelihood of your being hired.

Politics and Competition at Your PhD Institution. Departmental politics in your own department may also spill over and affect your job-searching activities. In departments that are highly factionalized, graduate students may receive help from only one part of the faculty. You can try to avoid this situation by not taking sides in faculty conflicts and focusing, instead, on completing your own dissertation and work.

Especially in large graduate departments, politics influences which students are recommended for which jobs. Faculty members may develop their own favorites among the job candidates and may push their candidates over others. Sometimes departments centralize job applications to the point of trying to ensure that two candidates from the same department do not compete with each other by applying for the same job. Indeed, maneuvering through your PhD program and department may involve considerable skill, but such skills will likely be of benefit in your first academic job.

Your Personal Background and Assets. Your own background, training, specializations, and achievements will also affect your success in the job market. Strong letters of recommendation from senior faculty, finishing your dissertation, acquiring teaching experience and developing a teaching portfolio, and presenting and publishing papers while in graduate school will give you a competitive edge in the market. In the example at the beginning of the chapter, those were the main differences between the records of Paul and Mary.

You can improve your chances of getting an academic job by your own choices and actions, but all of these factors we have just discussed will have an influence on your success. Some of these you cannot control. Ultimately, however, your time and energy will be well spent emphasizing the things you can control. Those things most under your own influence are your coursework and success in it, professional activities, and research and teaching. Emphasize these in your approach to the academic job market, and you may be successful in obtaining a desired position.

2 | Searching for a Job

Given the scarce availability of academic jobs and the numbers of PhD candidates completing their degrees each year, candidates finishing their PhDs cannot assume (as they could 30 years ago, depending on the field) that a job will just fall into place. Thirty years ago, the availability of jobs often came to the attention of department advisers and they helped to arrange placements for each student completing a PhD, but this is no longer the usual pattern. The situation today is very different because the academic job market in most fields is tighter than it was 30 years ago, although it may not necessarily be tighter than it was at times 10 to 20 years ago. Three contrasting cases of PhDs from the early 1960s, late 1970s, and the early 1990s illustrate the shifts in the job market, as do the stories of Paul and Mary (also from the 1990s) in the first chapter.

In the early 1960s, when the academic job market was still booming from the growth of enrollment in college that began after World War II, Allen's search for a job was fairly typical of students from strong programs. He had graduated from a Top Ten midwestern school in sociology (probably a Top Five school in his specific area). During the year when he was completing the collection of data for his dissertation, he talked with his adviser about the type of place he preferred and the parts of the country he liked. His adviser asked whether he wanted to stay an additional year to finish his degree (the department had the funds) but he said he wasn't sure because he was recently married, and he and his wife were anxious to get settled in some ways. During the winter, his adviser received a number of calls about good jobs and placed several students who were further along on their dissertations. Then his adviser received a call from an Ivy League University. Allen was from New England and had expressed his greatest interest in returning to that region but to a research-oriented university, not a small college. The adviser quickly called Allen who agreed to apply for the job. He flew out for an interview a few weeks later, with one major concern. He was not confident of finishing his dissertation during the summer. Once Allen returned, the department chair called Allen's adviser who said he was confident Allen could finish his dissertation the summer after his first year of teaching if not the summer before that. Allen was offered a tenure-track, three-year contract, with a specification of a built-in raise if he finished his dissertation by the start of the second year. Allen was off to a successful career, completing his dissertation the summer after his first year of teaching in New England.

Frederick was an outstanding graduate student who, in 1977, was progressing appropriately in his studies of American history at a large state university. He was working hard but needed at least one additional year of departmental funding to finish his dissertation. His adviser had already told him, however, that 10 years before he might have been able to find a job and then finish his dissertation, but few places now considered such hires. Unfortunately, the state budget was not generous that year, and the department decided not to fund any candidates for an additional year. Not from a wealthy family, Frederick felt desperate. His adviser helped him locate a part-time junior college teaching position. Although he taught five classes a semester, he managed to finish his dissertation. By spring, he had been to several professional conferences to interview and written for jobs he saw advertised. He found no permanent job, taking instead a one-year sabbatical replacement job halfway across the country. His new department encouraged him, saying they hoped to receive funding for a permanent position the following year. Nothing became available, but in spring a faculty member became seriously ill, and Frederick was offered another one year appointment. By the next winter, nothing had become available (the faculty member's health improved and he returned to that slot) and in late spring, Frederick accepted a one-year sabbatical replacement on the East Coast. By then married, he and his spouse moved across the country. Frederick was very discouraged and had published only a few articles. The time and stress of job hunting and moving had hindered his ability to turn his dissertation into a book. During the next year, he became friendly with many people in his new department, but no permanent line opened up. His spouse now had a good job in the new area and did not want to move for another temporary position. He decided to sit out the year and work on his book. By the next spring, he still had no position. A friend in the department heard about a museum position, and, deciding that he and wife wanted to make a life in the community and not move around constantly, he accepted the nonacademic position in a permanent career move.

Rita started graduate school in 1988, studying psychology at a large, private university. People told her the academic job market was due for a big improvement as retirements started to occur. She did well in school and selected a dissertation topic. She also started talking seriously with her adviser, who pointed out that because jobs were still tight, she needed to have a very competitive record. Her adviser suggested that Rita work with her on another project in addition to her own dissertation so that she would have some coauthored publications by the time she was job hunting. The department had recently decided to offer some promising students an additional year of funding to improve their chances of competing for good academic jobs. Rita was one of those chosen. By the fall of her fifth year (the time of the annual meeting in her discipline), Rita was confident of finishing that spring and had three articles accepted, one of which was due to be published shortly. She interviewed at the meeting and systematically applied for many jobs. By winter, she had had two interviews, one at a very prestigious university and one at a large state university. She was not offered the one at the more prestigious university but was offered a tenure-track assistant professor position at the other university. They wanted an answer in two weeks. After conferring with her adviser about whether to wait and see if a better job came open, she accepted the position.

In the two cases of academic job candidates in Chapter 1, Paul and Mary, plainly Mary approached her foray into the job market with more foresight and planning (and a greater appreciation of the current market limitations) than did Paul. First, Mary had systematically tried to prepare herself to maximum advantage during her entire stay in graduate school, not just at the time of her job search. Second, she developed and executed a logical plan for her job search. She determined beforehand that she preferred a major research university, even if certain conditions such as money and location were not as ideal as those at other types of colleges, and she stuck to her criteria as the time to make a decision approached.

Paul, however, did not systematically think through what his assets would be, nor did he approach his job search as methodically. His more restricted search limited the number of interviews he was offered. In the end, his emotional ambivalence about leaving the urban area in which he went to graduate school, coupled with the limited number of options he applied for and the competitive nature of his field, left him empty handed as the job season drew to a close. Fortunately, his PhD institution was able to patch together another year of partial support and teaching on an adjunct basis for his own and other departments in the immediate area. But he had to delay the launching of his career and look again the following year.

All five of these examples illustrate how the times have changed; how a candidate begins to get a job now is different from the way it was 30 years ago. Jobs are more widely advertised today and searches more broadly conducted. Thus a completing, new or recent PhD needs to play an active part in finding his or her job. This chapter will discuss sources of job information, review job application strategies, and discuss how to construct your curriculum vita (CV) and job packets and how to obtain letters of reference.

Sources of Job Information

How do you begin looking for a job? Academic jobs are specialized (as are most professional fields), so you do not turn to the local help-wanted pages. In truth though, most disciplines have their equivalent of help-wanted pages. Most people in the department in which you are finishing your doctoral degree should know those sources. By the time you read this chapter, you will probably already know whether there is a separately published listing of jobs to which you have to subscribe (as in sociology), a listing of jobs each month in both the formal and newsletter type publications of your field (as in public health), or a formalized job booklet for members of an association (as in management) that comes out several times a year listing both jobs and job candidates for a fee. If you are not sure how it works in your field, find out now from your major professor, the graduate adviser, and other doctoral students.

If you are in an interdisciplinary doctoral program, the range of formally advertised sources may be broader. You may need to think through more carefully how your areas of research and teaching interests cut across applied and disciplinary fields and in which of these fields you would be seriously considered for a faculty position. For some people in a straight disciplinary program, you need to consider whether your interests have an applied component, whether you could be happy being (or even prefer being) a faculty member in an applied related field, and where you should find out about jobs in those fields. One publication, the *Chronicle of Higher Education*, lists jobs in all academic fields as well as most administrative posts in higher education. This publication comes out each week except for a few weeks in the summer and over the winter break. It is now being made available on Internet as well.

Published listings of jobs are one of the most important sources of job information, however. Often notices are sent to department chairs and graduate directors at the same time that the formal advertisement is submitted to the disciplinary publication. Most departments either post these announcements or place them in a job book. Reviewing those sources regularly may help you to begin your search early and may alert you to departments that would particularly welcome applicants from your program.

Other formal sources of job information include listings and formal job interviews at disciplinary meetings. In some fields, meetings may only be ways to find out about openings a few weeks before they appear in published lists. In these fields, attending the meeting will provide you with some additional information about potential places to apply. But in some other fields, such as economics and modern languages, the annual professional meeting is the critical site of initial interviews and most places do not invite candidates for on-site interviews that they have not already prescreened at the conference.

The age of electronic communication may be gradually changing the listing of jobs. A number of professional associations maintain electronic bulletin boards and mailing lists. People on the lists often post job notices as soon as they hear about openings in their own department. Interest groups and discussion forums (such as the health management forum for those interested in the practice and research of management in health care organizations) often post job notices from individual members. If you are not on Internet or familiar with the use of electronic mail, you might find another graduate student who can show you ways to look up these sources. This growing source of job information falls between the more formal sources and older informal approaches. Tapping into the growing network of electronic bulletin boards and mailing lists will help you find job listings and provide useful sources of information for other aspects of your career as well.

Informal sources include any contacts that faculty in your department have or that you may have already developed through professional meetings or contacts back at your former undergraduate program. Most jobs in today's market will be formally advertised, although sometimes by the time the formal notice appears many people may have already learned about the job informally or through mailings and have their applications in to the department.

Finding out about all the potential openings in your area for the coming year is clearly important. Thus it is useful to consult as many different sources of job information as are available in your areas, even though there will be substantial overlap between sources. Better to read about one job three times than to miss hearing about a job that fits you well or is in a location you have always wanted to try as a place to live. At some places, it may be an advantage to apply early. Some departments review applications as they come in, whereas others pile them up until the closing date. For those that review them as they come in, an early application may be more easily noticed than one that comes in on the same day as 35 others three days before the closing deadline.

Job Application Strategies

The Timing of a Search

As Chapter 1 indicated, academics often talk about the job hunting season. Although the specifics may vary from discipline to discipline, this is typically from fall through spring. Generally, except for last-minute replacements due to unexpected departures, most academic jobs are advertised long in advance. If a person left the department the previous year, most departments will try to have the ad ready to be placed in publications in the fall. Disciplines that have job newsletters usually have the thickest editions from October through February. If the discipline holds a summer meeting, departments generally try to have the formal advertisement ready by then and even if they do not have the final description ready, they will have an announcement of a vacancy at a certain level, with more details on preferred fields available later in the year.

Most departments hope to have their ads out from October through December, often with closing dates in mid-January to the end of February. For entry level jobs, students trying to finish their dissertations need to expect to spend substantial time drafting application letters and checking the brochures in the late fall. Then they can have a large chunk of time to work on the dissertation in the winter, always remembering the need to have a scholarly talk ready on the dissertation topic in time for on-site interviews. In those disciplines that do not use a midwinter (often December) meeting as an interim screening mechanism, interviews generally start in February (with some places that finish early trying to interview in January) and finish no later than the end of March. This allows time for all candidates to come to the campus for an on-site visit, the department to make a decision and write a letter of offer, and for more than one offer to be made if the first choice of the department does not accept. Most departments try to have an offer out and accepted before the end of the academic year.

Although this is the major pattern of job advertisements and interviews, others also occur. Because there is some mobility at each of the ranks each year, some jobs open up at a later time. If an academic resigns a job in February, the department may be able to rush approval through and have the job advertised by March or April and rush candidates in so that an offer can occur before the end of the academic year or even during the summer. These later jobs are the ones for which it is most important to follow informal searches and check notices sent to your department, because those sources can be contacted immediately, whereas formal ads in newsletters often take four to six weeks to appear. In these cases, jobs are often listed with no clear ending date and with a statement that applications are reviewed as they are received so that the department can legally begin to make choices while still receiving more applications. In these types of cases, by the time the formal announcement appears in the disciplinary journals, the department may already be selecting candidates to interview. By that point, your application will need to look particularly interesting to be added to the visit list. Having your application in as soon as you see these later jobs advertised is thus an advantage. This is not the only reason for ads to appear in February or March. As budget cutbacks and questions about the budget have become all too frequent in many state universities, delays may occur in acquiring approval to advertise a job. This may result in a late ad. The same situation also explains why you may see ads that hedge on the availability of the position, by saying "pending funding" or "pending approval."

Not all academic jobs follow these patterns. Generally, tenure-track positions in humanities and social sciences do. A whole different pattern occurs in the biological, health and physical sciences, where completing students typically go to a postdoctoral position before obtaining a tenure-track position. These positions often last for two years and frequently do not include a campus visit before the position is offered. Although postdoctoral positions are sometimes advertised early in disciplinary job listings, notices to departments are more often a major information source for these positions, and selection mostly occurs in the spring, seldom earlier.

In some of the more crowded fields in the humanities and social sciences, especially in areas in which there are many more graduates each year than new tenure-track openings, you may have to apply for more temporary positions first (but not formal postdoctoral positions). These include one-year sabbatical-replacement positions and instructor lines that departments may acquire if they have a growth in majors and need more teaching or if a faculty member has moved temporarily to an administrative position. Often, deans provide these positions because they are temporary and carry no commitment of permanence if the enrollment or financial situation changes. These positions can help new PhDs gain teaching experience and make themselves more attractive in the next year's job market. To have this help you obtain a tenure-track position, you generally need to begin to publish articles and develop a research agenda at the same time. The difficulty of this is that often these positions require more teaching than tenure-track lines and the impermanence makes it hard to begin a new research project. Thus these positions are obviously desirable if the alternative is driving a taxi but may be less desirable than receiving continued departmental support for another year. This is especially true for students who may not finish by the start of the next academic year. Increasingly, many positions (including most postdoctoral positions) are contingent on your finishing the dissertation. If you do not, you will have major problems. With a regular faculty appointment, the rank and salary are often reduced to instructor level. Worse yet, you may acquire at the beginning of your career the negative reputation of having a problem completing your dissertation.

Because there is a season for academic job hunting, doctoral students need to think very seriously about how close they are to finishing, what their sources of support are if they do not obtain an academic appointment for the next academic year, and how to position themselves to be competitive for the upcoming year during that summer and early fall. You probably should talk about this with your adviser, as well as make your own judgment about how close you are to finishing. The adviser may have a different opinion. A letter from your adviser saying you are unlikely to finish, after you have sent a cover letter with your application saying you will finish by the end of the summer, will convince departments that you are unrealistic and probably not on good terms with your adviser, both bad impressions to create. Also, if the adviser knows you want to be in the job market during the year, helping you to finish your dissertation may become an important priority.

Your adviser (and possibly the graduate dean) is in the best position to advise you as to whether the department has the funds to support you for another year. A number of years ago, departments would often support for an additional year a student who did not find a job that met the department's expectations for that student. Increasingly, however, departments now may have clear, formal rules that students who enter with a baccalaureate degree will be provided with no more than four years of funding, and those who enter with a master's degree no more than three. In some cases, the rules may have an escape clause (in some of the social sciences for example, an additional year may be provided if the student collects original data rather than using large national data sets). Other departments allow no exceptions. If your department has formal rules, you probably already know them. If you are not sure, check right away so that you have a sense of your range of options. The smaller your field and the more specialized your areas of interest, the more important this is, because some years may be bad years in which few openings occur for assistant professors in your specialty.

Where You Should Apply

A range of different questions all relate to where you should apply. To what kinds of institutions should you apply? Do you know if you have preferences about the types of students you teach? Do you have strongly held geographic preferences (or preferences about the size of the place in which you live)? Will you feel safer with many applications out versus only a few? How competitive are you and how hard do you want to work over the next five to seven years? What is your strength—written communication or verbal presentation of ideas? Will receiving many rejections (a certain outcome of a large number of applications) depress you and make you unable to concentrate on finishing your dissertation? Answers to these questions will help you determine the kinds of places to which to apply, whether you should apply only in selective situations or very broadly, and whether you will rule out certain institutions because of geographic or living preferences.

What types of institutions did you go to for your under-graduate and graduate work—large or small, private or public, liberal arts or comprehensive? At the beginning of graduate school, you may have held in your mind an ideal type of job, perhaps returning to a small liberal arts college such as the one at which you were an undergraduate. One aspect of socialization in graduate school is that graduate school faculty are themselves committed to large, research-oriented positions. Socialization pushes you to making such a career choice yourself. If you still are interested in a small private college, be sure you have thought through the career implications and your strengths and weaknesses. Except in the case of the most prestigious small private college, it is difficult to make the transition from that kind of job back into a research-oriented university. Also, although most colleges and universities now have a renewed emphasis on teaching, generally a faculty member at a small private college both teaches more (compared to a university) and is judged more for promotion and tenure on teaching. You need to enjoy teaching and having contact with undergraduates for success at a small college. Also, there may be more expectation of availability on campus and working with students outside the classroom during the academic year. If this is what you want, you may need to make that clear and possibly even pursue such options against their advice, if your graduate school faculty are very committed to all their students going to prestigious research-oriented universities.

Some job candidates are very committed to public institutions and prefer not to have to deal with trustees and the vagaries of private funding. In truth, the differentiation between private and public is probably less critical these days. Publicly funded universities have been subjected to at least as many shifts in the funding level (in these cases, due to varying allocations by the legislature). The more important questions are whether you prefer a big, medium-sized, or small campus. Also, how much is research emphasized versus teaching? You can find smallish (under 5,000 students) publicly funded colleges with a teaching emphasis as well as large state universities with more focus on teaching. What are lacking are private colleges and universities comparable to urban universities such as Wayne State in Detroit or the teaching-oriented systems such as the state campuses scattered across California. At both of these types of institutions, most classes are large and the social class background of students, their age, and their prior academic preparation are very different from students at elite private research-oriented universities or liberal arts colleges. At the major campuses of state universities, although the faculty are very research oriented and some students outstanding in their prior academic achievement, there is typically more variation of academic ability and achievement than in the most elite private universities. Class sizes at the public campuses tend to be larger as well. Research and publication emphases, however, will be stiff at the major campuses of state university systems. For the private, research-oriented universities with the best national reputations, there may be pressure both to be an outstanding teacher and an outstanding researcher as well.

Before beginning to send out job applications, it's helpful to try to reflect on your own strengths and weaknesses as well as the balance you hope to obtain between career-related aspects of life and a personal life. At the most competitive private and public research universities, the years as an assistant professor will mean very long hours and pressures to publish, obtain research funding (depending on your field), and increasingly be at least a competent if not a good teacher as well. Try to match your goals, strengths, and aspirations to the demands of the particular departments and institutions to which you are applying.

Think through the types of places where you have lived before and the kinds of activities you enjoy in your leisure time. If you are a city person who wants to be able to view foreign films as soon as they come out and have a diversity of ethnic restaurants nearby, working at a medium-sized state university in a small college town far from the urban population centers of the state may be frustrating. By contrast, if outdoor activities are your major form of relaxation, especially hiking and being able to commune with nature, taking a first job in New York City may put you in a place where you are unable to engage in the activities you enjoy and to relax enough to be a productive faculty member. Increasingly, your interests are not the only ones that count. Many graduate students are married or in long-term relationships and have a spouse or significant other who needs a job—those may only be available in metropolitan areas, making the more isolated college towns less appealing or even unrealistic locations.

These last few paragraphs should help you think through your more idealistic choices. You then need to balance those with the realities of your own situation and your own field. Are there very limited numbers of tenure-track openings each year? If so, you probably need to apply to all the ones you and your major faculty advisers feel are possibilities for you, even if you dislike the location or some are small teaching-oriented colleges and you had hoped to be in a department with a graduate program. The tighter the job market in your field and the more restricted your area of expertise, the more you probably need to apply to all the jobs that seem to fit you or that you have a chance for.

One additional consideration may be that some departments prefer not to have five graduates apply to each opening and try to coordinate the number of candidates who compete with each other. Although you may not always agree with these efforts and because you need references from the faculty, it's good to cooperate with these efforts as long as you do not feel that you are being discouraged from applying to any of the places you strongly prefer. On those occasions when you do strongly prefer the location and type of school or know you would be very competitive for that job, you may need to indicate that you are applying to that job, even though you understand that other students in the same department are also applying.

Other factors may also make you apply to places that do not fit your desires in certain ways. If you know you need (or very strongly prefer) to stay in a certain metropolitan or geographic area because of a spouse or significant other or an older relative needing care, then you should apply for all the jobs in your discipline in that geographically limited area.

The last aspect of where to apply is partially a strategic question and partially an issue of how comfortable you are with different kinds of circumstances. You should apply for all of those jobs in your discipline, in the type of institution you prefer, and in areas you are willing (even if not eager) to live. But some people feel safer by having many applications out, even though they know that it will lead to many rejections and mean applying to some places where they would make a weaker match. If you feel better applying to many places, do so. An important cautionary note is that you should not apply to more places than your references are willing to write to and talk to. Also, do not apply to jobs so far from your discipline area that you look ridiculous. Nor would you want word to come back to your current institution that you are applying to places unrelated to your background or unrealistic considering your achievements. Some people take rejection much harder than others—although you need to learn to live with rejection in academe (most articles are turned down, at least initially; most grants are rejected on the first round), you do not need to place yourself in a situation where opening the mail each day for a month or so depresses and discourages you from working on your dissertation. As with so many aspects of the job search, being good at analyzing your own strengths and weaknesses and the way you work, will help you in conducting a successful job search.

Preparing Your Vita and Cover Letter

When you apply for an academic job, you are always asked to submit your CV. These are the academic names for what is called a resume in business. If you have worked at a non-academic job previously, however, the norms about preparations of the two types of documents differ greatly. The goal of each is to present what experience you have had and to paint yourself as favorably as possible and make yourself stand out as a candidate to be interviewed. In resume writing, however, brevity is stressed. In an academic CV, the tendency is to include more rather than less information and brevity is not the desired goal (although padding is not a good practice either). Resumes are typically only a few pages. If you are a beginning faculty applicant, your CV may be that short but in 10 years it will be much longer. Also, CVs generally do not include a Career Objective section that describes the type of position a person wants. It is assumed that you are aiming for a tenure-track faculty position, with expectations (in varying degrees) of being a teacher, a researcher and a good citizen of the college or university community.

Appendix A has an example of categories often contained in a CV and the placement order of such categories. There are a number of publications that include more examples of sample vitae, some specific to field (the example in Appendix A is generic and should be applicable to most fields), and these should be consulted for more details (Anthony & Roe, 1984; Heiberger & Vick, 1992; Lewis, 1988; Rice, 1986). This chapter includes some general guidelines and hints. Often, the career planning and placement service at your university may be helpful, although these services are generally oriented to helping students find employment in business or government and at the bachelor's or master's level, not academic employment. But they may have an expert to help in resume writing who is also partially knowledgeable about academic CVs. In any case, they often may help with proofreading and suggestions. Some placement services stress quality of paper and variations in type to make a resume more appealing. In general, these tricks are less often used in CVs and may even make some faculty members distrustful of the candidate's understanding of academic norms.

To write your vita, you must review your educational and professional background and have appropriate dates and information ready to be included. There is some variation by field in what people expect to see in a vita, and checking with your own adviser or the graduate adviser and students that have been in the job market previously are good things to do before you decide your vita is finished enough to be sent out as part of a job application.

Certain material is in all vitae. The essential list includes your name, current address and telephone number (preferably both home and office), review of your educational experience, review of relevant prior professional experience, publications, scholarly presentations, and academic and research-related honors. If you have already received some external funding for your research, that should also be noted. Other types of things often included on a CV are relevant extracurricular and community activities, professional memberships, service with professional associations, foreign language skills, and selected personal data. Increasingly, academic CVs of people in teaching positions or applying for such positions list areas of past teaching experience or teaching competence as well. For finishing doctoral students, often a vita may include a two or three sentence synopsis of the dissertation topic and the name of your major professor.

Usually the personal information is at the top of a CV, as shown in Appendix A. An important consideration for current graduate students is to include a phone number that is answered in daytime hours. Invest in an answering machine. Including a fax number or e-mail address is increasingly useful. For reimbursement purposes for on-site visits, it is helpful to have the social security number included.

Debate continues about whether personal information such as gender, age, minority status, and family information (marital status and presence of children) should be included. For most of these categories, it is now illegal to discriminate on the basis of these characteristics. In fact, many departments have situations in which if they find a qualified minority candidate, they may be able to receive an additional faculty line or what have become known in some universities as "targeted opportunity lines." The truth is that some of this information can work for or against people depending on the situation. For most younger job candidates, age is not a major issue. Some returning students or ones embarking on a second career believe that departments are reluctant to hire 50-year-old assistant professors. Often, however, departments can figure this information out if they want to badly enough, especially if the returning student completed the bachelor's degree when much younger. Minority status for Hispanics and Asians may be assumed (correctly or incorrectly) from last names, and gender is usually assumed from the first name. The pieces of information most controversial are the family data. Many women believe that departments assume a married woman candidate (and especially one with children) is less serious. If you believe some of this information will lower your chances of being interviewed, do not include it. More and more CVs exclude family information, although the birth date is frequently included.

For foreign students, a related issue is information about visa status (not shown on the sample in Appendix A). If it indicates your availability for employment, include it. If the situation is complicated, it is probably better addressed in a letter or at a later stage in the job search process. If you are a U.S. citizen but something about your background may cause someone to question that (such as foreign degrees), you may want to list your U.S. citizenship or your place of birth.

In the education section, you must include all the colleges and universities you have attended and degrees awarded. For more junior candidates, this is often the section in which to include your dissertation topic and the target date for its completion. Do not forget honors, although if you have enough these may be included in a separate section. If you are applying in a professional school, be sure to include professional experience and licensure or certification information in fields such as nursing, architecture and education.

Publications and presentations are the most important part of the CV for most faculty members. As your career develops, most faculty keep an up-to-date list of their articles, books and presentations by constantly updating their vita (this task is much easier today with word processors). For a beginning faculty member, your list will probably not be long. It is acceptable to list articles as submitted or even in preparation, but these are not a boost to your chances in the same way that several actual publications are. Do not pad your CV with presentations to a local group under scholarly presentations or listing an article in a newspaper or student newsletter as a publication. Prestige hierarchies exist in most fields, and many departments are negative to a candidate who they fear does not understand this aspect of academic life. Listing non-scholarly work as though it is scholarly may convey that impression. If you have only a few articles published, a committee may obtain them and read them even if you do not submit a copy. If you participated in the publication of an article as an undergraduate that is unrelated to the kind of work you do now, you may or may not want to include the article. It does indicate some writing ability and unusual initiative, but it may convey an inaccurate impression of your areas of interest.

For most faculty applicants, one CV should work for all applications. If you are in an interdisciplinary field and applying for positions in two different types of departments, you may want to tailor your CV for each group. Tailoring your application letter for each job, however, may be more useful.

You should always include a cover letter with your application and it should be specifically written for each position. A form letter sent to many institutions creates an impression that you are not that interested in the job and not very confident of your ability to obtain an academic position (and thus are applying to too many places to send individual letters). The appearance of the letter is important. Be sure it looks neat and contains no misspelled words. Letters for beginning positions do not need to be long, a page or so will probably suffice. For a more senior faculty member, the letter may contain more details and specify unique aspects of the person's career or special qualifications for the position. A sample job letter appropriate for a beginning assistant professor position is included (see Appendix B at the end of this chapter). It is a page long and mentions a few unique aspects of the person's background (relating to applied undergraduate experiences) and some of the specific areas of teaching listed in the ad. A letter from someone who has been in a tenure-track position for five to ten years would probably be longer and might include more explicit discussion of a research trajectory.

Generally, the first paragraph of a letter indicates what position you are applying for and how you learned about the position. The second paragraph (and more if needed) highlights a few of your achievements or special qualifications. Try to highlight the main interests of the job ad and show how you fit the job particularly well if you are responding to a detailed announcement. In the sample letter, the person mentioned her applied experience and linked it to her experience with teaching, because she was applying to a large state university where she had heard there was growing emphasis on teaching and concern that new graduate students often had never taught and could not relate to undergraduates. Different comments might have been better if the ad had stressed high research expectations and a part-time commitment with a research institute on campus. Sometimes ads are very short and include few specifics. In these cases, your letter will probably be more general. Sometimes a very general ad indicates a lack of consensus in the department about areas of greatest interest, however, so it is still useful to mention additional areas of teaching or research interest that may not be clear from the CV (perhaps because they are different from your dissertation topics and current publications). Often this section of the letter discusses new research projects and areas of interest, especially for candidates past the dissertation stage.

A closing paragraph often includes the offer to send additional material if requested. Job advertisements vary in the material they request. If an ad specifies names of references and sample writing materials, you should include them at the time of the initial application. In the example, Jane included a separate sheet with names and phone numbers of references. (Often departments call references once they have decided which candidates they are interested in. Including the phone numbers is a helpful thing to do.) The ad may request a dissertation abstract or syllabus of a course. In visual fields, a portfolio or slides may be requested. Try to include all things requested. It is probably not helpful to include such things if they are not requested, because the department will probably screen candidates on the basis of the CV and letter and then request more specific information. Some institutions now require a transcript, to ensure that candidates are accurately presenting their situation. If this is requested, do include it or indicate that you have asked to have one sent.

References and Letters of Recommendations

One of the most important aspects of your job packet is the part you have the least direct control over—letters of recommendation. Although you cannot control the content of the letters, you do play a major role (especially as a graduate student applying for your first position) deciding who is contacted. For beginning applicants, it is hard to overemphasize the importance of your dissertation adviser. Depending on the nature of the field, you may be strongly identified as his or her student and all jobs will contact that person first for a reference. The better known the person is and the more enthusiastic about you they are, the better your chances of landing a good academic job. Moreover, a strong adviser will help you get to the stage of being a job applicant by helping you pick a manageable topic and set realistic goals for finishing.

The better the relationship with your adviser, the less critical the other references are (because you can expect that letter to be outstanding), although most places will want three references. It is better to list specific people than let a prospective employer call people they know personally or have heard of in the department.

Who else should you list besides your dissertation adviser? One common approach is to list the other committee members on your dissertation committee. If you were an outstanding undergraduate student and have kept up a friendship with faculty from that institution, listing one person from there helps to establish a pattern of hard work, intelligence, and success. If there is a very well-known scholar in the department but not in your direct area, but you have had some contact with him or her (through a course, for example), it may be helpful to have a well-thought-of, very recognizable name on your list of references. Such people are often very busy, however, and you should check well in advance whether the person is willing to be a reference for you. In fact, you should check about the willingness of each person to have his or her name listed as a reference, as a courtesy, even though you should be able to assume that your dissertation adviser will provide a reference.

If you have already presented papers at meetings and had a positive response about your work from the session organizer or discussant, it may be useful to list someone like that as a reference. It is assumed that faculty in your own department have a vested interest in having their students obtain good job placements—in a very important way, your success in obtaining a good job also reflects the success of the program. One reference from outside the department is often viewed as a sign of strength and as more honest than relying only on faculty from your own department. Another way to receive a reference from a different university may be through contacts in professional associations. In some fields, such as in sociology, many of the subject area sections have a student member on the council. If you have served in such a role or on a committee, ask one of the officers of the section (especially if their work has some relationship to yours) if they are willing to read a paper of yours and be a reference for you.

If you do not list a specific person besides your dissertation adviser, the department or search committee chair at the place where you hope to be hired is likely to call your department chair and possibly the graduate adviser. Some departments will call these people even if they are not listed, so it's always best to at least have them be mildly positive about you (which may well be the case if you are not in their area and they do not know you well).

Suppose your relationship with your adviser is not the best or that you get along with him or her fine when working on your dissertation, but you do not agree on the types of jobs you should be seriously considering. Either of these situations is very difficult. If your relationship with the adviser is bad enough, you may need to consider a change if that is still possible. If not, you will have to try to counter that person's less than enthusiastic letter with very enthusiastic ones from other faculty. If you are applying for jobs in small colleges and your adviser recommends high-pressure research universities, you need to have serious conversations about this issue. Try to convince him or her that your reasons are valid or at least that you understand the implications of your choice. If your reason is based on fears of your not being able to compete at the level of certain places, you may want to listen closely to your adviser's opinion of you. If it is based on a lifestyle choice (you want to have a family soon and be in a less pressured setting, or you love teaching and do not have the same enthusiasm for the pressure of acquiring grants in certain fields), it may be difficult to convince the faculty adviser but see if you can agree enough for the faculty member to send supportive letters.

What if you are unsure of what your relationship with your adviser is really like? The person may be so formal (or so friendly to everyone) that you are not really sure of their opinion of you. Thus you do not know what they may say. The best way to deal with this is to try to have a good conversation in which you try to find out how supportive of you they would be and the types of jobs and universities they consider more attainable positions for you. Often, a very formal person will respond well to such a conversation and you will leave more confident of the type of letter that will be sent. With the more informal and friendly professor, you may encounter a puzzled look and attitude. Of course, they like you, think well of you, and would say good things. You might need to try to ask more pointed questions—how would you rank me in this class or with the students who have worked for you the last few years? And again, find out what jobs they think are the more attainable positions for you. If these conversations do not relieve your anxiety, one other approach is possible—we shall now discuss this.

A very difficult situation arises when you receive a hint that an adviser's letter is not that positive or contains some ambiguously worded phrases that make people question whether they should interview you. How can you confirm this or, on the other hand, establish that the person is writing reasonable letters? There are some ways, although they verge on the unethical and probably should be a strategy you resort to only if you have strong reasons to suspect problems. In the past, for example, stories abounded through student culture of faculty members who routinely wrote about female graduate students that they were attractive and bright but they doubted their commitment to a career over the long run. Or letters would emphasize the teaching, nurturing aspects of a female or minority student even when the career goal of that person was a research-oriented position. If you are in that situation, see if an undergraduate professor now at a different institution or a former graduate student at a department with a job opening is willing to look at letters written for you by that faculty member and advise you whether you should no longer use them as a reference. Do not ask them to send the letter to you, for that is clearly a violation of professional ethics and of the norms of confidentiality that the faculty member assumed in sending the letter.

A different option available at some university career and placement services is assembling a packet and leaving it on file. Often, those letters are available for viewing by the candidate unless you sign that you will not look at them. This may give you a clue about what the person says about you, although they probably realize you can view the letter and may change its content.

Often, it is a good idea to have a backup file of letters at the placement office even if your department generally writes individual letters for each job. This is especially true in a large university where people may leave for sabbaticals and research opportunities and you may not be able to reach them and acquire a new letter each time. One cautionary note, however, is that most departments do not evaluate these letters as positively as individually written ones. If you know an important reference for you is on sabbatical in the fall outside the United States and cannot provide individual letters, you might indicate that to the department at the time you list the person as a reference. It will save each place unnecessary phone calls and help to moderate their lack of enthusiasm about a placement-center letter rather than an individual letter of reference.

Concluding Thoughts

We hope you now have a clearer idea of how to find out about a job opening, select jobs to apply to, and construct a strong CV and letter as part of the application process. If you have a good relationship with your dissertation adviser and other faculty in the department, listing references should also work out well. As with many career decisions that will occur in the future, it helps to be somewhat self-reflective and able to assess your own strengths and weaknesses. It also helps to have a good understanding of when you are likely to finish your dissertation if you are still a student. Following these suggestions could lead to some departments having an interest in hiring you. The next chapter discusses the next intermediate step to being hired—the job interview. This is the critical next step for obtaining an academic position.

APPENDIX A

Sample Vita

Curriculum Vita

Name: Jane Doe   *Revised:* December, 1994

Home Address and Phone   *Business Address and Phone*
16 Cherry Lane   Department of ??
Seattle, WA zip   Big University
(804) 222-2222   University City, State zip
                                    Phone number

Date of Birth: Month, Day, Year   *Place of Birth:* City, State

Social Security Number: xxx-xx-xxxx

Education:
University   BA degree   Year
                                    Area of study

University   MA degree   Year
                                    Area of study

University   PhD Degree   Year
                                    Area of study

Positions Held:
Years   Rank and title, name of
                                    university and its location

Membership in Professional and Scholarly Organizations:
List associations

Honors and Other Special Commendations:
Scholarly honor societies
Best paper awards
Best presentation awards
Competitive scholarships
Student teaching awards

Areas of Research or Scholarly Interests:
Main areas and plans for future research

Description of Teaching Activities:
Courses have taught or are willing to teach

Description of Service to the School and Community:
Committees served on in university, graduate student associations, or professional associations

Publications:
Books
Articles and chapters in books
Abstracts and book reviews

Unpublished Thesis and Dissertation:

Grants and Contracts:

Conference Participation:
Papers presented
Programs arranged and chaired

Sample Job Letter for Beginning Assistant Professor Position

October 18, 1994

Professor Steven Jones
Search Committee Head
Department of XXXX
Big State University
University City, XX zip

Dear Professor Jones:

I am enclosing my CV for consideration for the junior faculty position advertised recently in the disciplinary job newsletter and the *Chronicle of Higher Education.* I am currently a graduate student in the Department of X at Known Private University.

As is partially indicated by my CV and my current dissertation topic, I am very interested in research on family- and child-related issues. However, I have also read and completed an area of expertise in organizations as well and thus would be interested in future research and teaching both in the area of family studies that your ad mentioned and also in the area of complex organizations that your ad mentioned. I have some applied experience in those areas as well, since I completed an undergraduate internship in a family social services agency. In fact, it was that applied experience that helped convince me I wanted to go on and study this area in further depth. I do believe, however, that my applied work experience will help me as a teacher and make me able to provide concrete examples in class.

Certainly, that has been the case in a weekly discussion breakout section of a large class on family sociology in which I have been the assistant for the past two years.

My enclosed CV further details my academic background, meeting presentations, and beginning activities in professional organizations. Your ad requested the names of three references; their addresses and phone numbers are given on a separate page. I have also included a three-page synopsis of my dissertation topic, a chapter from the dissertation, and a paper I will be delivering this spring at a regional professional association, since your ad requested writing samples. If further materials are required, I would be happy to provide them.

Sincerely,

Jane Doe

3 | The Job Interview

One of the most crucial stages of any academic job search is the job interview. Although in some disciplines, this can be a two-step process with one interview conducted at a professional meeting and a follow-up at an on-site campus visit, in most disciplines the meeting interviews are extra and not essential, whereas the campus or on-site visit is crucial. Very few people obtain academic positions (other than a one-year temporary appointment or sabbatical replacement) without an on-campus interview. This chapter will discuss what generally happens during the visit, what you should ask for and know before you go, what you should know about required presentations, when to ask difficult questions, and what to know about the role of dinner and other social obligations.

Preliminary Stages

Although in most disciplines, the on-campus interview is often the first occasion when you will meet anyone from your potential new department in person, most national meetings and some regional meetings do provide job placement services at their meetings. At smaller meetings, this may simply be a booklet listing job openings and job candidates. In other disciplines and meetings, the service may be very formal. This may include a way for employers and employees to review job and candidate information, to leave messages for each other and a physical location where interviews can be conducted. Often the job placement services are in a room different from that where the major portion of the meeting takes place. In a few disciplines (such as economics), doing well at a conference interview is the critical first step in finding a job. However, this is not generally true.

Interviews held at professional meetings are generally short (under a half hour). In many fields, these are low-risk but useful opportunities to test out potential jobs and have the places test you out also. If you do well compared to others interviewed, you enhance your chances of obtaining an on-campus interview. Some members of the department are likely to return to campus and talk about how bright you were, how well you fit the job, how far along you were in your dissertation or whatever it was that convinced them that you were an unusually appealing candidate for that department's position. If you do not make a great impression, although it does not advance your cause, it may not hurt it that much either. If you irritate a few people, however, or they are convinced you are very far from finishing or not serious about the department, you may then hurt your chances of ever progressing in that particular job search.

A typical convention interview consists of one person or a group of two to five people from the department. Generally, they have a set series of questions to ask each candidate and may interview 10 or more people during the course of the meeting. You should go to the meeting with a good supply of your CVs and enough to give one to each person while being interviewed. If you have a one- or two-page summary of your dissertation, bring some of these along as well to leave with the departments that interest you.

Time is limited, so you will make a better impression if you have answers to common questions already clear in your mind:

Will you have finished your dissertation by the start of the next
academic year?

What are your plans for submitting articles for publication from
the dissertation?

What direction do you expect your research to take in the future?

What areas of teaching do you want to work in and what could
you handle if you had to?

What has been your prior experience with teaching?

What are other special strengths and interests of yours?

Other issues often talked about include the following:

The teaching load and expectations for faculty

Your familiarity with the institution

Your familiarity with the department and the kinds of students
they have

The kinds of activities you like when not working

Your familiarity with that part of the country (especially if it is
quite different from where you are currently located)

If scheduling of interviews occurs at the meetings, it may be
difficult to have enough time to go easily from one to another.
If possible, try to avoid scheduling several too close together.
In these types of interviews, times often become delayed. If you
have three or four scheduled together, you may be late to
several and you will appear harried. If you miss an interview
because of receiving a note late or having another appointment
running over, try to contact the person and reschedule. If this
is not possible at the meeting, let the person know by a letter
afterward that your failure to appear does not indicate a lack
of interest in the job.

Often, departments may indicate an interest in meeting a
candidate at times other than when the interview room is
available. Breakfast or lunch meetings sometimes occur. These
may be longer, but you need to be sure to convey the essential
material and gain as much information as possible, even

though eating. If you are requested to meet over drinks, it is probably best to stick to soft drinks or slowly sip one drink. Be aware of the impressions you may make. Also, some people may prefer to interview in their hotel room, but some candidates are uncomfortable with such a meeting place. If so, you might suggest the lobby or going to have coffee or tea as an alternative. Always act in a way that maintains your dignity. If an interviewer becomes too personal or you are sure you are not interested in the position, try to leave graciously by indicating another appointment or that you are not sure you are a good match for the job and you do not wish to waste any more of the interviewer's time.

General Description of a Typical On-Campus Visit

Initial Planning. Most on-campus job interviews last two days. As the time for interviews approach, you will need to be able to get away for two- to three-day periods to do interviewing. If you have teaching obligations at your university, try to structure them in the fall so you can have more flexibility for interviewing in the spring. If this is not possible, you need to plan ahead so that you will be able to make visits to campuses. Perhaps other student teaching assistants can cover for you. Failing that, talk to your adviser about how this can be handled.

Although some departments will provide your ticket and pay at the time for the expenses of the visit, other departments will expect that you purchase your ticket and pay for the hotel room in advance and then will reimburse you afterward. With the wide availability of credit cards, having money up-front is less of a problem than in the past. You may find that your credit charges become large while you wait for reimbursement.

Meetings With Faculty and Other People. For an initial appointment as an assistant professor, you will probably have individual appointments with each member of the faculty. You may meet with some graduate students or possibly undergraduate students at smaller liberal arts colleges. Expect to have a meeting initially with the department head and another meeting with the same person at the end of the interview. One setting in which you formally interact with many people is at a research presentation. In some departments, there may be a more formal meeting with the search committee. Search committees may include a student or a member of a different department as well as a subset of department faculty. At other places, a meeting with a formal search committee as a group is not held. At most places, you will meet with a dean or an equivalent position holder in a small college. When interviewing for a senior position, you might meet the provost or president.

Social Events and Meals. Most visits include some social and meal events. These are less formal times. At such times, some more personal questions may be raised after everyone feels more comfortable. These types of settings also provide a different type of situation for you and the department to judge each other.

Often, the department chair may meet you at the airport and have a light supper with you initially. Alternatively, the chair may meet you alone for a breakfast the first morning. At that meal, the chair will explain your schedule and may talk about what different people are like or what some of their concerns are. Questions may arise about your interest in the position, whether there is a partner to help place, and when the dissertation will be completed. If you have not already been provided with a catalog, description of the graduate program, undergraduate majors, and listing of the faculty and their interests, some of these materials may be provided at this first meal.

Other social events vary. Some departments are very social and (especially if they are larger and there is no way for everyone to have a meal with you) may plan a cocktail party at a faculty member's home or a reception after your colloquium. In others, there may be a lunch that the whole faculty attends or, in a small department, a dinner that includes spouses. In a larger department, you will probably have different meals with different groups of people so that everyone has a chance to talk with you more informally.

Campus Tour. A tour of the department offices generally occurs. At some places, you may also receive a tour of the campus, the library, and special computing or laboratory facilities. You may receive a tour of the general area and different kinds of neighborhoods. The next sections will describe the questions to think about before your visit and details of parts of the visit.

Things to Ask About, Know About, and Be Able to Answer Before the Visit

It is helpful to obtain as much advance information as you can about the university and department prior to the visit. At the time you plan the visit, ask for a catalog or brochure on the department and more information about the faculty and teaching programs. Asking for more information shows interest. It may also help you decide how serious you are about the position. Reading material before you arrive on campus will help you be better prepared to answer questions during the time of the interview. A set of questions often arises about the time frame for the decision process and the visit. Although candidates are generally curious about the whole process, many schools are reluctant to indicate how many candidates are being interviewed and the detailed time frame of the whole process. You do have to negotiate a time for the visit around your schedule if you are teaching and also around the absence and presence of critical people in the department and the university. Sometimes in negotiating visiting dates, you may acquire a sense of whether you are an early or late candidate. If you suggest several different times for a visit and the department states those are already taken, it probably indicates that you are not the number one or two choice.

Asking questions creates a positive impression, but many types of questions are considered inappropriate until the department raises them with you. The following are good things to ask about:

General background and interest of the department
More information on faculty and their interests
Backgrounds of the students at the university
Backgrounds of graduate students
Current teaching needs of the department
Research interests of current faculty

Inappropriate or sensitive questions to ask about over the phone include the following:

The salary
The teaching load
The requirements for tenure and promotion
Availability of travel money and other amenities

It is unlikely that these issues will be discussed over the phone. It may take the full two days of the interview for details to be discussed. Rarely is the salary for a beginning position discussed over the phone before a campus visit. Sometimes if a department thinks they pay very well and that may convince a candidate to visit, they will mention the salary range on the phone. Similarly, some schools that think they pay poorly may also mention it over the phone, because they do not wish to waste limited interview money on a candidate who will turn them down on that factor alone. However, some departments may ask if you have a desired salary range. It's good to know the overall range of pay for the field adjusted for the cost of living in that area. If you are already in a faculty position or recruiting for a more senior position, it is more likely (but not typical) to have current salary range or salary expectations discussed at an early stage. If you have concerns that the teaching load is too high for you to be productive, you might ask a question about the relative emphases of teaching and research on the campus. This question might prompt an answer that includes a discussion of the nature of the university. An example would be a comment such as, "You know we are an undergraduate teaching-oriented institution, so of course, it's not surprising we teach a seven-course load a year." Sometimes if a college has a high teaching load, the department chair may tell potential candidates over the phone to make sure the department does not waste limited interview money by bringing a candidate onto campus who will no longer be interested once the teaching load is explained.

For current graduate students, you will likely be asked a question about the status of your dissertation before the visit is confirmed. You should have a ready answer for this. Some schools will be very explicit about the dean not being willing to offer a job to someone unless they are through. Other will point out that any letter of offer will specify a different level of appointment and salary if you are not finished by the arrival date on campus.

Meetings With the Faculty

To some extent, these can be grueling experiences. In a large department, you may have 20 different meetings with individual faculty of a half hour each over two days, answering the same sets of questions over and over again. It's important to stay enthusiastic as you talk about your research and career interests even the eighth time in a day when you repeat your background, interests, and goals in life. You can almost guarantee that every conversation (including those with the department chair and the formal search committee) will address certain topics: your dissertation, your future research plans, your teaching capabilities, and why you are interested in this institution.

Dissertation Questions. This is often the first area of questions if you are still in graduate school. You should have clearly in your mind a paragraph length answer to the question, what is your dissertation about? You should first answer that question and then be prepared to follow up on their questions about the topic after your initial explanation. If you are meeting with someone very knowledgeable on the topic, it will be clear quickly. If you know they are doing work in the same area, you can say, "I am sure you are very familiar with some aspects of my dissertation research, so I hope we can talk about it in more depth after I give you a few facts." You should expect to explain the major themes of the dissertation, why you find the topic interesting, and why the topic is important. Some people may also question you about how far along the work is and whether you will be finished before the position starts.

Future Research Plans. This will probably be the first area of questions if you are already through your dissertation and the second set of questions if you are still in graduate school. If you are still in graduate school, although it is good to talk about plans to split the dissertation into articles, you also need to talk about future research plans. Departments are always concerned that the potential faculty member will not really be able to work on his or her own and come up with new research ideas. If you say you haven't thought much beyond the dissertation, their fears for your future productivity grow. If your research requires funding, it's good to be able to mention sources from which you will initially try to obtain funds. For people already in a faculty position, you need to be able to talk about your current research plans and also give some indication of how those might be enhanced if you were to move to this particular job.

Teaching Interests and Experience. Teaching is increasingly important on many major campuses and has always been a central concern on liberal arts campuses. You should expect to be asked questions on what you might want to teach. It's easier to do this if you have already received and reviewed materials on the department and university. Then you can mention specific courses already offered as well as list areas of personal interest for which you did not see courses listed in the catalog. Be sensitive about appearing as though you will be unhappy unless you teach certain courses if you know you are talking to the person who currently teaches those courses. Some faculty are very possessive about the courses they teach and may worry about you as competition, fearing that their own role in the department may be diminished or they may have to prepare new courses. In such cases, you might point out your related interests and say that you would enjoy teaching certain courses if they were available but also could teach some others. A delicate balance is called for, because it's likely that someone teaches most courses listed in the catalog. If you mention only courses not being taught by the department, people may decide you are a bad fit. But if several faculty do not want to have to change their teaching assignments and fear that you would push to teach the courses they prefer, you may lose needed votes and support among those faculty. If few courses in your current area are offered, you can discuss how you might hope to build more departmental strength in this area, but also remember to point out some of the existing courses that you could cover.

Why do you want to be here? This question can be troublesome. If you are a beginning faculty member interviewing at a strong department or university, the question is usually not problematic. But if you are interviewing at a mid- or lower-range state school or a smaller, less distinguished liberal arts college, you need to indicate what is attractive to you about the place, even if the major attraction at the moment in a crowded job market is that it is a tenure-track appointment. In this situation, you have to strike a balance between offering glowing comments that come across as false versus insulting the people who are currently on the faculty at the institution. Faculty who remain at an institution for a long time develop some commitment to it and generally regard it more highly than people viewing it from the outside.

Related to the questions about the institution are issues about the geographic area in which it is located. Sometimes people in smaller towns or parts of the United States traditionally less popular in academe (southern states, midwestern states, mountain states) are concerned about the dangers of recruiting people only to have them leave in two years. If you have lived in this part of the country or this size area before (perhaps when you were a child and your parents were moving for various jobs) and it is not clear from your CV, mentioning that is always useful. A comment such as, "I really enjoyed the three years my parents lived in a similar midwestern town when I was in elementary school" tends to put everyone at ease when they realize that, even though your CV indicates mostly East Coast experience, you have a fond memory of the Midwest. It gives them confidence that you might be happy in this location.

Why do you want to leave your current job? For already employed faculty members, this may be one of the most difficult questions. But if you are already on a faculty at another university, the issue of why you are leaving will probably be raised. You need a consistent answer that emphasizes the attractiveness of this place and new experiences, rather than focusing on problems at your current job. If there are some important reasons for leaving that relate to structural issues at your current place of employment, discussing those may be appropriate and not place you in a negative light. Examples include a desire to work with colleagues who have similar research interests if that is a strong point of the new institution and a drawback where you are currently. Sometimes people want to move because they dislike that part of the country or have concern over potential budget cutbacks. You might mention these, because they are not problems you personally have with your current institution. More difficult are those situations in which you are looking for another job because you have been turned down for tenure, or fear you will be, or those in which you have conflicts in your current department. In general, most faculty are very leery of hiring another department's problems, so mentioning difficulties getting along with other faculty members or advisers is not a good thing to do at an interview. If you are up for tenure during this interview year, you may want to mention that given budget concerns or a new dean or other changes, you and the other faculty are less confident of how tenure decisions may turn out and you have decided to use this year as an opportunity to explore other options as well. Generally, most faculty will already know about your situation (especially in a small field or if the two schools are in the same part of the country), so you need to admit the truth and the fact that you do not yet have a firm tenure answer. If you have already been turned down for tenure at your current institution, the department has probably heard that. It is best to admit that you will not remain at your current institution and then focus on the attractiveness of this institution. Do not dwell on what went wrong in your application for tenure or denigrate the department you are leaving. It makes you look negative, and departments want to hire a positive person.

The Presentation

Often, the single most important part of the on-campus visit is the formal presentation or talk. The presentation, especially if it covers scholarly material, is a way for the department to judge the quality of your scholarly work, how well you convey ideas in an oral setting, and how quickly you think on your feet as you answer questions. The presentation is the part of the interview many job candidates fear. Part of the fear relates to past negative experiences at the current graduate institution. This is particularly true for candidates from institutions in which oral defenses of dissertation proposals turn into settings in which different faculty members each try to show how they can find missing ingredients in the proposed research. Generally most departments are more polite to potential job candidates than they may be to PhD students in their own department. The other aspect of fear and concern about the presentation is real, however: A good presentation may increase your ranking as a candidate, whereas a bad one may lower the department's interest in you.

Typically, especially for a junior candidate, the presentation is about your dissertation research. If you have already published an article on a different topic, you might propose that topic also and see if the department has a preference, although often departments will also use the talk to gauge whether the candidate will complete the dissertation before beginning the job. You should begin working on a talk before you have any visits scheduled, because the first interview may be scheduled in a very short time frame. Although the thought of this presentation may be daunting, remember that you will know more about your dissertation topic than anyone else. That should be a boost to your confidence.

Some smaller colleges now request a different type of talk or may ask a job candidate to lecture to a class in addition to making a scholarly presentation. If you have never taught before, running an undergraduate class for an hour with little prior feel for what they have covered can be a difficult situation. You might suggest a topic linked to your dissertation, but be certain that you lower the level of the material to be appropriate for the audience. If you have been a teaching assistant and prepared some lecture material before, you may want to present that and just update the material and perhaps include more audiovisual aids and perhaps more opportunity for student interaction than you might normally. If you are going to talk to a class in midsemester, request a copy of the syllabus, try to talk to the instructor about what has already been covered, ask about the background of students in the class, and find out whether or not the instructor generally allows questions throughout the period. Presenting an undergraduate class lecture that is well received is often more difficult than presenting a research seminar on a topic you have been immersed in for years. Given a choice, most people are probably better off to opt for a more traditional research presentation format, unless you have prior teaching experience and know that you can shine in this format.

Sometimes, a department may ask if you have a preference about which day or the time of day a presentation is scheduled. People differ on whether they prefer to give the talk first or whether they would rather have met many of the people in the department and have a better feel for them.

You should be able to obtain information about the nature of the talk and who typically attends. This will help you customize the talk slightly for each interview. Find out who is likely to attend (faculty and graduate students at a large university, faculty from this and other departments in a smaller place, or only departmental faculty). This will help you determine how much background you need to present. Be sure to include some of the actual data and analysis if this is appropriate to your topic. Try to present material in a way that would indicate you will finish with your degree by the time you start the new job. For example, we have seen presentations where the candidate focused on measurement issues in the data or general theoretical approaches rather than the larger analysis. Sometimes this backfired, because the department interpreted the lack of overall results as an indication that the job candidate would not be finished for the fall, even though the person's adviser was confident of this.

Some of the same recommendations apply for this presentation as for any professional presentation (see *How to Make Effective Presentations*, Tierney, 1996, in the Sage series, for more general tips on presentations). Try to have readable overheads or enough copies of your handouts to go around. Carry your talk and these supporting materials with you on the plane, in case your luggage is lost. Pace your talk, leaving enough time for questions at the end. Speak clearly and distinctly. If you are very nervous (and if you have not given many professional presentations, you may be), it can help to admit that in a joking manner. Have some water available to sip. Very important, it helps greatly to practice the presentation at least once with other students or your adviser and hear their critique. Have them ask you questions. You will do a better job answering a question if you have already tried to do so before. Remember phrases that help you stall for time while you think: For example, "That is an interesting question." "Could you explain your question a bit further?" If you really have not thought of certain implications you are asked about, then you may want to admit that they could lead you in a different direction from the one you were considering before. You might go on and indicate that you appreciate the idea and may be able to incorporate it in one of your final chapters or future articles.

If the presentation does not go as well as you want (it was too long, someone asked hostile questions, you had difficulty handling the questions), try not to dwell on it and have it ruin the rest of the interview. If others comment about it to you, indicate that it was one of your first presentations or some other mild explanation. If substantive questions arose about the research, you may have a better answer by the next day and might want to explain that to the major questioner.

Dinner and Other Social Obligations

Dinners, lunches, and cocktail parties and receptions can be very important occasions for you and the department to learn about each other. It's natural that you may be nervous in these situations (it's not the typical dinner), but try to relax and be natural. Also, pay attention to the different people in the department in this setting. If it is a party, can you see cliques forming or do people socialize with lots of different people easily throughout the evening? At a dinner, you can tell a lot about whether the group socializes in general or whether this is an unusual occasion because of the job interview. Often, people will spend part of the conversation talking about things other than you and the job. If people are catching up on each other's lives (as indicated by statements such as, "I haven't seen you the whole year"), it's probably not a department that socializes much with each other. It is useful to have a better feel for what obligations and expectations about socializing with the department may be, and these social occasions will provide such cues if you are a good observer.

Follow the lead of the others on whether you are talking about the department and the discipline or more general topics. Do try to interject some things about yourself when appropriate. Be good company and sensitive to the general conversation. If you are naturally shy, you still need to try to talk and convey interest in the department and the people. Try to talk to everyone during the time of the reception or party. At a dinner, if you did not get to talk to someone much, make a polite comment about being sorry to be unable to chat more and suggest speaking the next day. Do not drink much at these events, although ordering a drink or wine if everyone else is, will probably give them a better sense that you fit in with the group. People do judge each other on appearances, so watch your manners at meals. Clothes even for social occasions should be generally professional and on the conservative side for the whole interview process. Men generally wear a suit or slacks and a jacket in a more casual place. Women wear dresses, suits, or a skirt with a jacket. It might be good to take one more casual outfit, in case the department suggests a visit to a very casual local restaurant (such as a barbecue place in Texas or the South).

Forgotten Items

Sometimes faculty candidates can spend two days on campus and realize as they are leaving that, except for general impressions, they did not learn any details of the new positions. They do not know the teaching load, the salary range, or the time frame for the decision. Look at your schedule closely once you arrive. If you have a meeting with the department chair at the end of the visit, this is the time to raise these issues. If you do not see such a meeting scheduled, you may want to ask the department chair or chair of the search committee if there will be a time before you leave to talk about teaching responsibilities, the time frame of the search, salary and other issues of importance to you (computers, office space, etc.). The way to bring up issues the chair does not clearly cover is to ask whether the department has a typical or expected teaching load and how this would apply in your case, if you came.

It's also a reasonable question to ask about the process for the rest of the job search and when you might hear from them again. Sometimes, especially for beginning faculty positions, you will receive a clear answer. "You are the second of three candidates we are bringing in and the last one comes in next week. We have a faculty meeting scheduled the week after your visit and I expect to get back to candidates shortly after that." Many places try to hedge on information about this, however, because if you are not their first choice, but their first choice person turns them down, they can offer the job to you without it being clear you were second choice. More details on negotiations connected with offers are included in Chapter 4.

Problematic Situations

Sometimes you may be asked sensitive or troubling questions by faculty in the department. The most troubling ones are often those focused on personal situations. Although many questions are now technically illegal (asking if a candidate is married or plans to have children, how they handle any physical disabilities), people often want to know these things and it is important to try to answer the underlying concerns calmly and professionally. For example, a woman who is herself undecided about having children might simply respond that she is very committed to her career and would continue to pursue her career and research plans whatever personal decisions are made. A question about how old a person is when addressed to a job candidate who is older than the norm for a beginning position could be answered by talking about how much you think your prior life experiences will enrich your teaching. You can stress how you have learned to plan your life and understand how you work best and that these skills will help you be a productive faculty member. Some of these situations are difficult because you may need or want aid (you have a spouse and need help in job placement for him or for her; health insurance specifics may be very important to someone with a physical disability). In those cases, it's good to bring some of these issues up fairly early in the interview.

Concluding Comments

Job interviews are stressful. We hope this chapter has given you a better sense of what may occur during the interview. Being prepared is helpful, and we think that some of the tips and ideas from this chapter will help you be successful in your interviews. One of the most difficult parts of the job interview occurs once you return home—waiting. One way to benefit from past interviews is to review the experience in your mind soon after you return (before the details fade). If you had trouble answering questions about your research or future career plans, think about what might have been better answers for the future. Make adjustments to your presentation. Then get ready for the next interview.

4 | Landing the Right Job

Between the job interview and actually beginning a new job comes a sometimes trying and long period in which you wait for an offer and, after receiving one, negotiate a deal. This period is crucial to your final success. This chapter will review most of the major issues and situations that arise as part of negotiating the details of an offer. Although there is great similarity across many job interviews, negotiating a deal varies more. Thus this chapter covers some of the most typical issues that arise after the campus interview is completed and before a contract is signed. These include issues of timing, focus on salary and details, and the meaning of verbal offers versus signed contracts that specify details. The chapter also reviews some factors to consider when choosing a job.

Negotiating a Deal

Issues of Timing

Do not assume from the length of time that has passed since the interview that you know what is going on. After you have been on an interview, the length of time before you hear again from anyone at the college or university may vary considerably.

Several factors influence how long this period is, including how much of the academic job season is left, your position in the sequence of campus visits, whether or not you are the department's first choice or the department is in conflict, and institutional procedures or constraints at that institution. If it is late in the academic job season and the hiring department is anxious to wrap up its job search before faculty members disband and disperse for the summer, you may hear relatively quickly after an interview. You may receive a call a few days or a week or two after your visit making an offer. If it is still early in the season, the hiring department may feel under less pressure to conclude its search and may take longer to come to a decision. In this situation, weeks (or in rare cases even a couple of months) may transpire before you hear either positively or negatively from the hiring department. The best thing to do in this period is to continue to work on your dissertation if it is not done and on other projects, as there is nothing else you can do to improve your chances.

Your position in the sequence of campus visits does affect the length of time that transpires between your own interview and subsequent contact with the hiring department. If you were last in the sequence, the search committee and hiring department could rapidly move to make a decision after your departure. But if you were early in the sequence and the interview process stretches out over several weeks, it may be a long time before you are contacted. Some departments will contact you in the interim, just to ascertain your continued interest in the position and whether you have taken a job elsewhere, but other departments do not.

If you were the hiring department's first choice, you will hear sooner, perhaps even with a verbal offer or hints of one during your last contact with the department chair before concluding the visit. If you were not the hiring department's first choice, obviously they will make an offer to the first-choice candidate before approaching you. Because this offer to the first-choice candidate takes time to obtain university approval, and time again for waiting to see whether it is accepted, this is one of those situations in which the whole process becomes very slow. If the first choice turns the department down, which could take a month from your visit, then the hiring department has to reconvene, decide on either a second choice candidate or extension of the search, and have the new offer to you approved.

Conflict in the hiring department can slow down or even stymie its progress toward a hiring decision. Recognizing the tremendous importance of making a new hire, departments with a tendency toward dissension may have disagreement among the members over which candidate to hire. In such circumstances, the department may opt to bring in additional candidates but may not have definitely rejected the early candidates. Thus the passing of a long period after your interview does not mean that you will not in the end be made an offer. Rather, the department may have decided to search more broadly due to disagreement over what characteristics a good job candidate should have.

Institutional procedures can also affect the time required for the process of approval. In large universities, the approval processes can be long, requiring multiple sign-offs before even a verbal offer can be made. Sometimes key personnel who must approve a faculty appointment are out of town, also causing delays. In some instances, funding for a position that was initially there may be jeopardized if budget cuts materialize or appear imminent. Fears of a temporary freeze on new hires due to budget cutbacks can sometimes speed up a decision or may lead to further delays as deans refuse to make decisions.

During the time period when you are waiting to hear whether or not you have an offer, the tendency may be to leap to the conclusion that you have been rejected. But do not assume you have not been selected until you actually hear this from the hiring department. Any of these circumstances could also be at work, affecting and frequently lengthening the time between your campus interview and notification of the appointment decision by the hiring department.

Being late in the sequence of campus interviews is probably better than being early. At the time you are invited to a campus interview, you may not know where you stand in the sequence of candidates visiting the campus. If when the search committee chair called you, you were given wide latitude, of say, a month and a half during which to schedule your visit, the likelihood is high that you were the first candidate being called. If you picked an early date, the time frame of waiting to hear will be more extended than if you were the last person to visit. Is there any position in the sequence of campus interviews that works to your advantage in receiving an offer? Although some would argue that being early in the interview sequence is preferred, because you have the chance to be the first to make a positive impression and therefore impress faculty who may be anxious to focus on a viable option, most faculty members will likely withhold judgment until after seeing all of the candidates. Being last in sequence means that you have the opportunity to make the most recent and vivid impression in the minds of the search committee and other faculty before they go to make their decision. Being last also means that faculty may be less likely to nitpick over characteristics of your candidacy they do not like. If you appear early in the sequence, some minor characteristic that the search committee does not like and finds less than optimal may be sufficient to cause members to discount or devalue your candidacy. If, however, you appear late in the sequence after others have been discounted or devalued, minor flaws may appear less fatal, particularly if there is pressure to bring the search to a conclusion. Being last generally does mean you will hear sooner, because most departments try to complete the hiring process fairly quickly after the last campus interview has been completed.

Try to structure your interviews so offers are likely to come close together. In landing your ideal job, you may be presented with a dilemma if your first invitation for an interview is at a college in which you are less interested. Plainly, until you have a job, you cannot afford to turn down interviews that may lead to one. But if you go on interviews to schools that are low preferences and are offered a position, then you are confronted with a difficult choice. Do you turn down a sure job because it is not among your top priorities, to await a possible interview and offer from a school of higher priority? Or do you take an offer from a school lower in your preference ranking because you are not sure you will receive an offer from a higher ranked school?

The dilemma is even more acute if you have received an interview invitation to a school that is a top priority, but the interview is sufficiently late in the academic season that you are likely to have been made an offer from a less-preferred school you visited earlier in the interview process. To the extent that you can, you should try to bunch together your interviews so that you are likely to be made offers from competing schools close together. Bunching interviews may mean that you get very tired and weary from almost back-to-back campus visits. But it may result in your knowing whether or not you will get an offer from various schools at about the same time. Even if colleges vary in how long it takes to respond, which we just indicated is likely to happen, if the interviews are bunched and you have already been interviewed, you are in a position to call that school and inquire how the process is progressing and where you stand if you receive a competing offer.

Focusing on Details of Salary and the Position

Do not appear to focus on the perks and benefits of the job until after you receive an offer, but focus instead on salary and major concerns such as teaching loads and responsibilities. In strategizing how to land the job of your dreams, one tactic is likely to backfire—that of focusing in great depth on the perks and benefits of the job before you have the offer. It is acceptable to ask some questions about benefits and perks, but most questions should focus on the main duties, workload, aspects of the program, salary range, and characteristics of the department and institution. Some questions about pensions, health benefits, tuition waivers and reimbursements for yourself and family members, travel money, and other benefits are OK, but to dwell on these subjects at length is not helpful.

A better strategy is to find out as much as you can about the salary scale of your discipline and the college before you complete the negotiations. College administrators who determine what salaries should be for various positions that are being advertised are likely to be aware of what beginning and average salaries are for your field, by rank. So should you. Knowing typical salaries for your discipline helps you be realistic and pragmatic as you receive an offer. The more you know about compensation in your field, the better off you are likely to be in stating what your salary expectations are if asked and in knowing if an offer is high or low compared to others.

How do you find out information about such a sensitive subject as salaries? Some state universities are required to publish annual salaries and place the document in the campus library. The likelihood you will know this on a campus visit, however, and have time to go track down the document, even if it exists, is not great. In some universities and colleges where a report containing salary levels for faculty does exist, access to the document, even though it is in the library, is tightly monitored. You must know where in the library to go, must sign out the document, and access may be allowed only in one room. Thus it is unlikely and probably not politically wise to try to accomplish this on a campus visit. If your own campus has such a volume, perusing it may be help you to acquire a feel for current salary ranges in some places, adjusting for the cost of living. Otherwise, talk with your faculty adviser, other faculty members and other students searching for a job, to obtain their impressions of beginning salaries. A published source of information is available in the *Chronicle of Higher Education* and AAUP (American Association of University

Professors) surveys of colleges and universities, which yearly publish salary information, by institution and by rank. But this is not specific to discipline, and disciplinary variation is quite large.

In general, larger universities with advanced graduate programs pay more than smaller liberal arts colleges or state colleges without graduate programs, but not always, especially at beginning levels. You are less likely to have input into salary negotiations at beginning levels than you are at mid-levels or senior levels in the discipline. At the top levels, a recruiting institution may be prepared to offer what it takes to obtain the candidate of their choice or may have an authorized spending range. At the beginning levels, a department may also have a hiring salary range, but the range will be narrower. Sometimes authorization to hire at a specific beginning level salary has been specified by a dean or provost, and the department has almost no flexibility to alter that amount. One problem to be aware of is salary compression. As market rates for beginning positions rise in some fields, within institutions where raises have been modest (this especially occurs at state-funded institutions), beginning assistant professors may be offered salaries that exceed those of other professors who have already been working at the institution for several years. This makes it important to begin at the best salary possible but can also cause interpersonal difficulties if your starting salary is close to or above that of an associate professor who has been there for eight years.

If you are unaware of typical salaries, administrators will sense that you can be bought for less than the amount they have budgeted and may offer you less. The money they save can be spent on other hires or other institutional concerns. Women have in the past been offered lower salaries than men. With equal pay legislation now in effect, differentiation on the basis of gender or race is not legal, but positions could be defined differently to justify offering lower salaries to some candidates than to others. In salary negotiations, as in buying used cars, the best advice is "caveat emptor"—buyer and job candidate beware.

Obtain as much as you can going into a new job because you will never have a better chance, but do not give up an attractive option over small differences. You will likely never be as attractive to the department that hires you or have as much leverage with them as you do when you are being recruited. Whereas it will appear unseemly to focus on perks and benefits before you receive an offer, after you receive one and before you accept is the time to negotiate any benefits you hope to receive. Things you might want to ask for include a computer and software relevant to your work; a teaching assistant or research assistant if the hiring department has these resources; a reduced teaching load the first semester until you get settled in; the opportunity to earn a summer salary through teaching, contracts, or grants if you are on an academic salary; and travel monies. Also, ask if your moving costs will be reimbursed and, if so, up to what amount. If you are in a field that requires scientific equipment, a laboratory, or both, ask for everything you need to conduct your research before you take the job.

Most likely, no job offer will be perfect. Some job candidates will receive only one offer, and others will receive none, at least on their initial foray into the academic job market. If you are one of the lucky candidates to receive more than one offer, how do you choose among the possible jobs you could have? Rarely will you have a choice between the perfect ideal job and one of lesser appeal. If you did, choosing would be easy. But the reality is most jobs have some characteristics or attributes that you do not like. Knowing that, it does not make sense to reject a job because of minor flaws or differences in amounts of money over what the hiring department offers and what you think you are worth. The perfect job may not materialize, and a job with minor flaws is a major improvement over being unemployed.

Verbal Offers, Signed Contracts, and Legal Issues

A verbal acceptance is professionally but not legally binding. What do you do if you verbally accept a job that is not your first choice, only subsequently to receive a better offer from a school you prefer? If you turn down the second offer, saying that you have already accepted an offer elsewhere, you will likely have twinges of regret for some time. But if you renege on the first offer to take the second, you could develop a reputation for being less than trustworthy. Plainly a pattern of repeated reneging on verbal acceptances will garner you a bad reputation. But some circumstances make reneging on a verbal offer more acceptable than others. One would be if a better job comes along that enables a dual career couple to be closer together or would allow both to get jobs in the same location. Another would be complicated personal circumstances, such as wanting to return to a particular area to help aging parents. In general, reasons that do not imply there is something wrong or inferior about the hiring department are more likely to be graciously accepted.

Other factors that will influence the hiring department's attitude toward you is whether or not they have other acceptable candidates who are subsequently recruited. But that is not something you are likely to know. How you handle such an awkward situation may also influence their attitudes, along with the time period between when you accept and when you decline the offer. If the time period is very short and if you call the department to let them know immediately, they may hold less ill will toward you. Faxes and other modern technological devices have reduced the time between a verbal offer and when you sign a letter of offer and subsequently, a contract. Overall, the best situation is to avoid ever reneging at all.

Obtain key aspects of the conditions of your job in writing, including clarifying of unusual situations such as interdisciplinary appointments. Remember, the written contract is the legal document. As previously discussed, at times fiscal exigencies or emergencies may cause hiring freezes to be placed on a position at the hiring institution. In other situations, a member of the search committee may overstate either optimistically or inadvertently the degree of support for your candidacy. Perhaps a new dean or provost at the hiring institution decides to take a department in a different direction, reshaping or restructuring the position for which you interviewed. Because of these and other possibly unforeseen circumstances, it is always better not to sever ties with your current job or department until you have a written commitment about the new job. Always wait until you have received a letter of intent and contract before you submit a formal resignation from your current position or relinquish funding in graduate school. On personal matters and professional relationships, it is also better not to alienate professors and colleagues at your current department until you are sure you are moving (even then, it's better not to alienate colleagues and professors at all).

You have negotiated a favorable deal with the current department chair that includes special benefits, such as computer, travel and moving expenses. Try and have all the important aspects of these arrangements in writing, preferably in the appointment letter stating the conditions of employment. These include whether or not the position is tenure track, the time frame for reviews, including renewal contracts and tenure and promotion, teaching loads, any guaranteed summer monies, and any moving expenses.

Across time, memories of the details of the deal may grow dimmer to those less affected by it than you. Having the employment conditions in writing prevents that from happening. Also, given the structure of universities, provosts, deans and department chairs may step down and be replaced. You will want written proof of the terms of the negotiations you conducted when you were hired. If the conditions are part of your appointment letter, they become legally binding, even if personnel shifts occur in the chain of command.

Sometimes universities will structure positions so that they are split between two departments or so that in addition to departmental commitments, part of a newly hired faculty's time is to be devoted to an interdisciplinary program. Such arrangements may be exciting, with great possibilities for cross-fertilization and intellectual growth. They are also fraught with possibilities for conflict and misunderstandings. When you work in two departments at the same time, each may demand more than fifty percent of your time. Each may expect you to have their interests as your primary concern. To avoid misunderstandings and to capitalize on the positive aspects of interdisciplinary arrangements, try to clarify both verbally and in writing the relationship of the two departments to each other and particularly to you. Your appointment letter should specify in which department your tenure (or tenure-track position) primarily resides. If possible, try to have a clear written understanding (perhaps in a letter from you to the chair or from them to you) of how much of your time should be spent in each department. Your teaching loads in each should also be clarified, to prevent each from demanding that you teach a full load.

Use competing offers to leverage very carefully. For job candidates who are already working, an offer from another institution may be used in some settings to leverage or to convince your current employer to raise your salary. This is done by obtaining a job offer with a higher salary from another institution, ideally of comparable or better quality than the one where you currently work, and taking the offer to your department chair or dean or both, to find out if they are willing to use the letter to negotiate a higher salary in your current job. If they counter the offer with a reasonable raise or improvement in conditions, then you have a choice as to whether to move or to stay where you are currently working.

Especially if your intention is not necessarily to move but rather to use another offer to raise your salary at your current college, then such tactics should be used cautiously. They may not work. Your current college may indicate no additional funds are available or only modest funds, so you are confronted with a choice now of staying for little or no extra money or moving and relocating for more money, but not necessarily to a department you prefer over your current setting. If you use the competing offer tactic to leverage, you should try to make sure that the offer comes from a school where you legitimately would like to work, as you may have to follow through on an implied threat to move if you do not get a raise.

In a slightly different version of this tactic, a new PhD first entering the job market may receive two or more offers almost simultaneously. The candidate may try to use the offer from a school that is less preferred, but that has made a higher salary offer, to raise the salary being offered at the other position. In essence, the candidate is trying to start a limited bidding war if the leveraging goes on for more than one round. Again, caution is advised, unless you are prepared to carry through with your threat to take the offer from the higher salaried school if the college offering a lower salary does not match it. Exercising caution does not mean never trying to leverage. Rather it means using a leverage tactic only when you think you can live with not getting what you want.

Factors to Consider When Choosing a Job

What factors are important to consider as you examine an offer to see if you want to take the job? Obviously no standard list can include all the issues that are of importance to you, but some standard issues affect the overall desirability of most jobs and shape candidates' preferences when selecting between offers. This section summarizes and reviews important considerations. These include both professional concerns such as the immediate conditions of employment (whether the position is tenure-track, the type of college or university, the salary, and the quality of students), the future potential of the job (compatibility with faculty, ability to conduct scholarly activities, the likelihood of getting tenure, and proximity to external professional opportunities) and personal aspects (geographic location and family and relationship concerns).

Immediate Conditions of Employment

Tenure-Track Position. In the hierarchy of job offers in an era when jobs are scarce, many universities along with corporations are downsizing in certain functions, and mobility among professors is low, tenure-track jobs are typically preferred to nontenure-track positions. A tenure-track position is one that carries with it the right to earn tenure. A nontenure-track position does not include that right. Whether or not a job is tenure-track is a key characteristic of the position that should be clarified before you take the job. It will affect your immediate treatment and expectations for activities in the department, not just your future. Teaching loads, availability of research assistance, and help with publication all may differ if a person is hired in a nontenured, heavily teaching-oriented position.

Departments are typically allocated a limited number of tenure-track positions based on student enrollments, program diversity and complexity, and history. A department cannot unilaterally decide whether or not to make a position tenure-track. Rather, it must receive a tenure-track position allocation from college administrators—deans, provosts, vice presidents, and presidents based on department needs and college priorities. Tenure-track positions are scarce resources over which many political battles are fought, especially given the trend within higher education to lower costs by replacing tenured and tenure-track faculty with adjuncts and part-timers.

You may take a position that is not tenure-track hoping that it will convert to a tenured position once you are there. Although some conversions of this nature have occurred, the likelihood of that happening is not great and certainly is not something on which to count. Furthermore, the conversion is not a function of how you are performing but, rather, of how well the department and institution are doing financially.

If such a conversion occurs, you may have an inside track to acquire the tenure-track position, but universities and colleges are typically required to conduct a national search to fill positions. Going to a tenure-track position is generally preferred to taking a position that does not include the right to earn tenure.

The Type of College or University. Most PhD candidates have preferences for the type of institution at which they want to work. Some prefer research universities with strong graduate programs. Usually such departments have larger faculties where teaching loads may be lighter, classes larger, research expectations high, and a high degree of specialization encouraged. Other PhD candidates may prefer smaller colleges where faculties are smaller, teaching loads higher but classes smaller, and breadth rather than depth is encouraged.

Salary. Everything else being equal, more money is preferred to less. A position with a higher salary is preferred to one with a lower salary. Furthermore, salary affects more than just the size of your paycheck. Because retirement plan contributions are typically calculated as a percentage of salary, the higher the salary, the higher your retirement contributions. At some universities and colleges, pay for summer teaching is also calculated as a percentage of base salary.

The problem when comparing offers is that other than salary everything else is often not equal. The salary offer may be higher because the position is located in a high cost urban area, where the additional money is more than eaten away in housing and commuter costs. And often, the position with the higher salary may have other characteristics you do not like, whereas the position with the lower salary may have other characteristics you prefer. You must balance how important money is to you relative to the other factors in making a choice.

Teaching Load. To some job candidates, having a light or at least reasonable teaching load is very important. Teaching loads may vary greatly across colleges and even across departments at the same institution. In many fields at major research universities, a two-two teaching load is considered normal. This means teaching two courses in the fall semester and two in the spring semester. In some departments and fields, teaching loads may be even less—three a year. At nonresearch colleges and some liberal arts colleges, however, teaching loads may rise to four a semester. Although research expectations are lower in the latter cases, often some research is expected. Beginning faculty may be able to negotiate an initial reduction in teaching their first semester or year to enable them to become acclimated to the university and to their new duties, although not all departments and colleges are willing to do this.

Another critical question involves what you will be teaching. How many new preps will you have your first semester and first year? The term *new prep* refers to preparation of a new course you have not taught before. Teaching the same course twice to two different classes is typically regarded as less time consuming than teaching two new courses. Having fewer preps is preferred to having more. Also, will all of the courses you will be teaching be in the major areas in which you concentrated your graduate school studies or in areas tangential to your studies? Courses where you have less training yourself obviously will require more work on your part and detract from time you can devote to the research you need to do to obtain tenure. Will you be given large lecture sections or small seminars? Large classes may be very time consuming if you must do all the grading of papers. But if you are given a teaching assistant to help you with grading and student problems, they may be less time-consuming than other classes that are smaller but have no teaching assistant. (See *Improving Your Classroom Teaching,* Weimer, 1993; *Tips for Improving Testing and Grading,* Ory & Ryan, 1993, for suggestions on how to handle your teaching load effectively and efficiently.)

Quality of Students. What is the quality of the students at the college or university where you have received an offer? For some job candidates, student quality is an important consideration. Students may vary tremendously in quality as measured by SAT scores and high school grades and rank, depending on the type of institution that is making you an offer. Undergraduate students with high standardized test scores and high school grades may be easier to teach in some ways but more challenging in others. Most faculty prefer teaching graduate students who attended demanding undergraduate colleges and who scored highly on GREs to those who did neither. Various compilations provide data on the selectivity of colleges concerning their student populations. If you taught or talked with a class as a part of your campus interview, you will then have some limited firsthand experience with the students as well.

Future Potential of the Job

Compatibility With the Department. A very important part of a new job is how happy you think you will be working in it. Do you think you will be compatible with the other members of the faculty, especially the senior tenured ones who will be voting on key aspects of your career, including tenure and promotion? Is your vision of the future similar to that of other faculty already in the department? Try to judge the department on this important aspect of compatibility. Great diversity exists among institutions of higher education as to their missions, student populations served, and self-images. Finding a position in a department where the direction of the department is compatible with your own goals not only will enhance your short-run comfort but also your potential for long-run success.

The Likelihood of Getting Tenure. Not only is finding a tenure-track position important, getting tenure is too. Once you have a job, there are many things you can do to increase your chances of getting tenure (See *Getting Tenure*, Whicker, Kronenfeld, & Strickland, 1993). But one of the best things you can do to enhance your chances of getting tenure is to pick the right job in the first place. The right job is one where the expectations for achieving tenure are similar to your own goals and match your capacity to deliver.

Being in a department where the expectations are far beyond what you can realistically achieve in the allowable time will lead to frustration and eventually, sometimes sooner rather than later, looking for another job. However, being in a department where your own expectations and capacities far exceed those of your fellow department members can also be disastrous if you threaten those faculty. A good match in the academic job market is when the expectations of the hiring department for subsequent performance and achievement are closely aligned with those of the candidate.

Proximity to External Professional Opportunities. Does your profession or discipline require on-site work or work in the field? Political scientists, for example, may benefit from being close to Washington, D.C. or to state capitals. Professors in health administration may benefit from being in a metropolitan area with many health care institutions. Geologists or archaeologists may need to be near certain field sites for their research. Music professors may prefer to live in a culturally vibrant center with many performing opportunities. Sometimes these external opportunities are crucial to building a research record that enables you to compete successfully for tenure.

Personal Considerations

Geographic Location of the Institution. Many years ago, a popular television western about a gunslinger for hire named Paladin was called *Have Gun, Will Travel* after the declaration of intent on the gunslinger's business card (yes, gunslingers, like professors, had business cards). A similar declaration by some of today's job candidates would read, "Have resume, will move." Some candidates are willing to move anywhere within the continental United States to obtain an academic job with tenure-granting status. Others will even move outside the United States. The *Chronicle of Higher Education* often includes advertisements for jobs at colleges and universities in other countries.

Other job candidates feel they must restrict themselves by personal preference or necessity to looking for a job in a particular geographic region. Such restrictions may rule out otherwise acceptable jobs (as was the situation for Paul in the scenario discussed in the first chapter). The larger the geographic location in which candidates are willing to search, the more likely they are to find a position.

Family and Relationship Issues. Especially in the era of dual-career couples and working mothers, family issues may be an important consideration in accepting a new job. You may choose not to discuss your particular family situation. But do you sense the department will be understanding of and sympathetic to your particular situation, including possibly the need to help a partner find a job? This issue is discussed in more detail in the next chapter.

5 | Dual Careers, Senior and Nonacademic Jobs

Much of the material in this book so far has been focused on the typical job search and is more oriented to graduate students looking for their first academic position. This chapter will deal with less typical situations but ones that many people find themselves in at some point in their careers. We will discuss three quite different types of situations. The first discusses jobs beyond the initial position and special aspects of moving at the associate or full professor level. The second part of this chapter raises the complexity of being part of an academic couple (or even just part of two people looking for jobs together even if only one is an academic). The third portion of this chapter deals with jobs that generally require academic credentials (a doctorate degree or a master's degree and coursework toward the PhD and often publications and grant experience as well) but are not located within universities. These include positions as consultants, in research firms (both profit and nonprofit) and even research positions within university think tanks or specialized research centers. Other related positions are those with governmental agencies, especially federal government jobs in certain fields.

Moving Up: Special Issues
for Associate and Full Professors

The more job interviews you go on, the more you begin to develop a feel for the process and think about what it takes to prepare for each one. Most faculty members who are at a more senior stage probably feel well prepared for the actual interview and the presentation of research. Some special issues do come up as part of the search for jobs at more senior levels. Even if you are beginning your first job search, understanding how some of these issues work in other job searches can be helpful and can help you have a better appreciation of the dynamics within departments.

Searching for a job at a senior level is fairly common. Although most academics who find a tenure-track job stay in those positions longer than academics did 30 years ago, many people will decide to look for another position after obtaining tenure and being promoted to an associate or full professor position. Sometimes people look to see what is out there or to increase their salary if they have been in a state system with salary compression and believe their current market value is substantially above their current salary. Other times something about the current job changes (a new department chair, a cutback in support for graduate programs at the university, or a new research emphasis of the department that is of little interest to you) and you may decide to look around. A third scenario is that of another department contacting you about a job or a colleague placing your name in nomination for a new position. Sometimes the desire to shift jobs derives from personal considerations such as a divorce or split-up with a life partner, a marriage or remarriage, or discontent with the city in which you live and with school opportunities for your children or career opportunities for your spouse or significant other.

Probably the most difficult situation for moving is as a tenured associate professor, especially if you have been at the associate rank for only a few years. Many universities will not accept someone with tenure at the associate professor level. So if something changes about your department and you want to leave in your second year as an associate professor, you may need to seriously consider whether you are willing to move as an untenured associate professor and have to go through the tenure process again. If you are not willing to do that, you may need to wait a few years until you have been promoted to full professor at your current university. More typically, moves at the full professor level do carry tenure with them, although depending on the system (especially at some of the more formalized state systems) you may have to produce a miniversion of a tenure file for review at the new university before the final offer with tenure appears in writing.

Moving without tenure is always somewhat risky. Some people do it, either because they dislike something about their current situation or because the new one is very attractive. If you decide to do that, be sure you understand what the rules are at the new university. Will you be put up quickly (in your second or third year)? In that case, you will be judged mostly on your previous work as long as you can demonstrate that you did not cease writing, research, and publication when you moved. Of course, your teaching that first year or two needs to be strong and without problems. Or does the university expect you to wait four to six years for a tenure decision? In that case, what will be the expectations for substantial new research and publications? The assessment of teaching will also be over a longer period of time, and there may be expectations of service to the institution as well as the overall profession.

Even at the full professor level, you should clarify that the new appointment includes tenure or that you will be put up in your first year. In recent years, some universities have become very reluctant to grant tenure at the time a person arrives. Many full professors, however, consider a move with tenure to be essential.

Some different questions will be asked of you if you are moving at a more senior level. If it is a regular faculty position (not a position as department chair or a named chair), some people will want to know why you are looking and why you are considering leaving. You will need to have a reasonable answer for this. Often, departments are worried that there have been problems or personality conflicts and they want to avoid bringing such problems to their own departments.

Another concern of interviewing departments is that you are just using the interview to obtain a salary increase at your home institution. This is often a major concern because it is a reality of academic life. In state university systems in the last five to ten years especially, raises have not occurred at rates commensurate with the increase in salaries at the beginning level. One of the few ways to obtain a raise is to have an offer from another university and then see if your own university will match the offer. This can be a dangerous game in several ways. First, you should be very careful about going to your dean or department chair with an offer to be matched from another university if you have no intention of taking the other offer or no desire to take it. What may happen is that the department chair says, "Sorry, but we have no additional funds and this would create an issue of salary inequity in the department. It does look like a great opportunity for you, though, so I am sure you will take it." If you do not take the other offer, then your credibility and stature in your current department in the future are probably diminished. If you do take it and are unhappy, you place yourself in the situation of wanting to look soon for another position and having other universities worry why you move so much or if there were problems you caused at the new university.

If you do look for other jobs but parlay those offers into salary raises at your current institution, you should be aware that you cannot do this time after time. If you interview often and are offered jobs but never take them, especially if your field is smaller, you will acquire a reputation for not being a serious candidate. Then, if you end up wanting to move in a few years, it may be more difficult.

Dual-Career Complications

An increasingly common phenomenon in academe is that of the dual-career couple, including partners who are both academics and partners who each have a career, one of which is academic.These couples are very often concerned about finding a job for the other partner as well. Whereas 30 years ago, most academic departments did not have to consider the issue of finding a job for the partner of the faculty member (the wife, in most cases, because most faculty members then were men), 10 to 15 years ago departments began talking about the issue of finding jobs for female candidates' husbands (because, of course, given the general societal image at that time, all husbands needed to find good jobs). Some departments even had to deal with the situation of partners who were both in the same field. Today, most departments consider this to be a potentially serious issue in any job search, whether the candidate is a male or female, because both male and female partners of the candidate are increasingly concerned about their own job opportunities in the new city. Women candidates are no longer seen as having a special problem in this regard, as compared to men candidates, but most departments are still delighted to discover a single candidate, one whose partner's company has already agreed to move the partner to the new city, or a stay-at-home spouse. Probably the most common reasons for candidates turning down job offers today are problems with finding suitable work for the partner.

What can you expect in the way of help from a department? When should you let a department know about your dual-career needs? How does this differ for beginning jobs versus more senior positions and those partners in the same academic field versus those in different academic fields?

For academic couples who are together in graduate school, looking for that first academic job is probably the most difficult challenge, because unless one of you has had astounding success in graduate school, CVs of different candidates look the most similar at the time of applying for the first job. When there are many people applying for this beginning position, why should the department bother to interview you if they know you will then demand help in placing a partner? In this case, the best advice (especially for two academics in different fields) is for each of you to apply to many different jobs (and all those within commuting distance of a job that the partner finds particularly attractive) and not mention the issue of a partner in the initial letter of inquiry. In fact, it's probably best not to mention it when the initial interview is arranged. If you expect help from the department with placing your partner, you probably do need to mention it at the visit, especially later in the visit if you think it has gone well. Some candidates fear mentioning a spouse at that point, because they are afraid the department will then lower them in the ranking. Although this may happen on occasion, if a condition of your accepting a position is having a job or a strong possibility of one for your partner, you should realize that it will take time for the department to help you in this matter, and in fairness to them, you should let them know right away. If you like the job so much you will move there anyway, then it may be good to delay mentioning the situation until the time of a verbal offer and then indicate you are definitely accepting the job but need help finding your partner a job.

This situation illustrates one of the most important rules for a dual-career couple as they approach the job market. You need to talk together and think through your strategies. Are you willing to have a commuter marriage and, if so, how far apart? Where you can each drive to the other's place each weekend or where you are on opposite ends of the continent and see each other once a month or less? You need to have thought through career issues for each of you. Will you move anywhere or concentrate the search in fewer parts of the country and larger areas with lots of different universities? If one of you is in a field with many more openings than the other, it may be best for that person to look the most and try to negotiate a placement with some opportunity for the partner. The other side of this picture, however, is that if your partner is in a field with few academic openings, this strategy will probably lower the chances of your partner ending up in a traditional tenure-track faculty job. If, however, the partner with the hardest-to-get job looks the most, that will mean lots of applicants for few jobs, and the person offered the job will probably not be able to convince the department to help that much with placement of the partner. Why should the department make this extra effort at the beginning level when there are so many candidates?

There is no better illustration of the dilemma of maximizing all goals than this—an academic couple trying to find first positions. It may not be possible to accept the best job offered and still live near each other. Couples have to decide how to prioritize what is most important. Moreover, couples will have to reassess these decisions at various points. Commuting by air up and down the East or West Coast may not be that difficult when you are each in your 20s or early 30s, focused on your career. If a couple decides to have a child or if one person develops a chronic illness, that arrangement may be much more difficult. Some couples get so bogged down in trying to plan their whole careers and lives together they become immobilized. You need to plan, but do it one move and one life stage at a time.

If your spouse is in the same field but can be placed in an applied field or another university, you may follow the same pattern as two academics in different fields. But if you are both in the same field and don't have that option, you may need to adopt a different strategy. If you both want jobs in the same department, it is probably better to be honest about that need at the beginning. Although your both being in the same field may facilitate research and communication in the household, it will probably complicate an academic career at the early stages. Departments often have only one junior position at a time. Some academics may consider sharing one position, but this opportunity occurs in few places. In all dual-career situations, but especially if you and your spouse are graduate students together at the same university, you need to talk to your advisers. Often departments will call the adviser, rather than the candidate personally, to explore whether the couple will move separately or if the partner will take a one-year sabbatical replacement appointment. If your adviser has not talked to you, he or she may give an answer different from the one you and your partner have agreed on.

What will a department do to help you? Departments and universities differ, and each situation is unique. If your partner is in a field different from yours but one generally under the same dean, the department may be able to help in placement within that university. If the department is very interested in you as the candidate and the dean administers the department of your partner, the dean can create a one-year position or even a permanent line if he or she wants to. The trick here is both how much the department desires you and the status of departments in relation to one another. A weaker department or one not expecting vacancies soon may be delighted to obtain a new position even if it means having a new department member forced on it. If the department is strong, it may react negatively to pressure. If the department is administered by a different dean, only gentle persuasion may work because the pots of money are separate. In a small college, the provost or president might create a new position. If your partner is not an academic (a lawyer, doctor, or in business), members of the department may be able to provide some help, but this will probably depend on the knowledge and experience of their own spouses and friends in the city.

For dual-career couples, it may be easier to move when at least one partner is more senior. That person will have a more sharply identified record and a department may be more likely to decide that they very much want that person and therefore will try to create a position for the other. At this stage, the creation of a second position for a more junior partner in the same department or college administered by the same dean will probably be easier. This may be true if one partner is still willing to accept a position as an assistant professor, but by the time the partners are both senior, moving together is probably not something that will happen quickly. Finding two tenured full professorships in the same department is not easy. Nor is it probable that a dean will create a tenured full professorship in a related department for the partner. Thus, at the senior level, finding two new jobs together can be a very lengthy process whether the couple is in the same field, a related field, or a completely different field.

For dual-career couples, several pieces of advice that apply to all academics are especially important. If partners need to coordinate their move, it helps if they each have a strong record and are somewhat flexible about what they most prefer to teach, what it really takes for their research to bloom in a particular setting, and where they wish to live. Trying to find a job is always stressful; trying to find two jobs definitely doubles (and perhaps triples) the problems. Couples need to remember that the job search should not be competitive between them, that maximizing the benefits for them both is the goal. Most couples with a strong relationship find something that works (although it often means a different career path for one person). For couples in weaker relationships, whose career commitments might outweigh the value of the relationship, each potential job move may require a decision that the career is more important than the relationship.

Research Positions and Other Special Circumstances

Most graduate students completing a PhD aspire to a tenure-track university position, but academic training can also prepare you for other career options. Some are research positions, and others may be positions with the federal or state government. These are less typical career choices; if you consider such choices, the important question is whether you view the job as permanent or a temporary one contingent on your obtaining a tenure-track position later. Advisers at many major research universities discourage students from beginning their post-PhD training careers in these types of positions. Their reasoning is discussed later in this chapter.

Research jobs similar to faculty positions can be found at universities or private research firms, some of which had their origins as university research institutes and then became independent (like SRI, which began as Stanford Research International). Others are independent but maintain strong relationships with academic units, both in the same city and across the nation. RAND Corporation, for instance, has strong links with UCLA. You can also find research positions in commercial research firms and in research divisions of major corporations. A major growth area is with firms specializing in doing environmental and archaeological impact assessments prior to development.

Research positions are more common in certain fields like the physical sciences, engineering and biology, and in the health sciences. They are frequently available in the more quantitative social science fields. In archaeology, impact assessment firms have been the major source of jobs for recent graduates over the last decade. These types of positions are less common in the humanities and the arts.

Research positions at universities range from those located in regular academic departments that may carry professorial-related titles (such as research assistant professor) to those located in special research institutes in rented buildings away from the major part of the campus, carrying a special series of research and administrative job titles (such as research scientist and senior project manager). The type of work and starting pay in these jobs may be very similar to that of an assistant professor except for the greater concentration on one or two research projects, the absence of teaching responsibilities, and less expectation of continued funding. These jobs are often advertised in the same scholarly meetings and job bulletins as tenure-track academic positions. In fields such as the health sciences, many researchers may start their careers in these positions. They may even spend most of their careers in these roles. If you want a research job with the flexibility of later switching back into a tenure-track position (probably at a different university), research positions within university settings most facilitate this, although well-thought-of research firms such as RAND are not dissimilar in terms of providing the opportunity to switch back in the early stages of your career.

One disadvantage of most research positions in universities is that they depend on obtaining grants of soft money in contrast to the hard money from state revenues or private university endowment funds. One's ability to retain the job often depends on having enough grant money. Although a new PhD would probably be working with an established research team initially, expectations of bringing in money as the major investigator will quickly increase after a few years of work. Obtaining grant funds is necessary to success in many science and health science positions, but the pressures are greater in the contract research firms. Also, the time allotted for publications is often less, making it more difficult to move back and forth between research and tenured faculty positions.

Expectations differ about the types of funding one obtains in university research settings versus for-profit research firms. Within universities, more of the funding is through grants from both the federal government and increasingly from private foundations as attempts to balance the federal budget are limiting the amount of federal dollars available for this kind of long-term research. The funding also carries with it expectations of publication. In many of the contract research firms, most of the funding is from the government through contracts involving specific requests for specific research products rather than general solicitations for research on a variety of topics. The research in such firms is often high speed and high pressure, with an emphasis on writing more proposals so that there is always enough funding coming in. Once a project is over, little time may be allocated to publication of findings. If one of your career goals is to publish, you may be unhappy with this aspect of contract research firms. If you are interested in retaining career mobility and being able to switch back and forth across research and tenure-track university settings, the lack of publications generally makes this more difficult to accomplish if you begin your career in a contract research setting. Although it is possible to move back and forth across research and tenure-track university positions, the more common direction of movement is from a university position to a research firm.

Two other career options that use your doctoral skills outside the university setting are consulting firms and major businesses. Most of these positions are technical in nature, either in physical sciences or engineering, biological or health sciences, or business fields. Some companies have large research divisions that operate more similarly to a university research setting. (Bell Laboratories in New Jersey was known for many years as an excellent research setting for serious scientists.) In others, research is the major focus but the emphasis is on production of new products, such as in the chemical and drug industries, so publication is not generally an option. Although these positions are often attractive in pay and benefits, movement back and forth into university research settings is not common in most of these jobs. In addition, you may need to explore beyond the more academic job newsletters to find out about these jobs. In the more professional fields, some newsletters generally cover both academic and nonacademic jobs.

Consulting firms are very important as a career option in business but also important in engineering and some of the more applied sciences. Although consulting jobs may be available to newly minted PhDs in business, more typically, people begin consulting careers after more experience has been gained in a university or research job. Consulting can be financially lucrative, although large amounts of travel are common in these positions.

The last different career option is in government, especially federal agencies. In the health sciences, for example, intensive research opportunities are offered within the internal research divisions of such agencies as the National Institutes of Health (NIH) and the Agency for Health Care Policy and Research (AHCPR). Similar situations exist in certain nonhealth sciences, such as the federal laboratories at Los Alamos, New Mexico, for physics-related research. At this level, movement between academic and government jobs frequently occurs. The concern over the federal budget, however, has limited growth in these kinds of positions over the last five years.

These positions are sometimes advertised in disciplinary publications, but the federal government also provides specialized listings and special forms to be completed to qualify for civil service positions. If you are seriously interested in these types of jobs, which can also be found in state goevernment, you need to fill out the forms and have your name listed as qualified within the appropriate job series. Despite the formal, open process, contacts do help. If someone at your university used to be with a federal agency or has a number of grants from an appropriate agency, having them call and obtain advance information about upcoming openings can be very helpful.

A related but different career track within government agencies entails work as research administrators in agencies such as NIH or as research interpreters and policy analysts in agencies such as the Congressional Budget Office or the Health Care Financing Administration. Although some people in these jobs leave for academic settings, most people who begin in these roles tend to stay within the bureaucratic and administrative sectors of the field. The longer one holds those types of positions, the less mobility one has back to academics.

Whether or not you plan to start your career in these positions, understanding some of the other options beyond traditional academic jobs can be useful. People's goals and situations change, and what is a less appealing career choice at one point may hold more interest to you later.

6 | The Do's and Don'ts of Job Searching

The cases of Paul and Mary discussed in Chapters 1 and 2 and the other vignettes described in Chapter 2 helped to illustrate some specific points of positive and negative strategies in a job search. This chapter discusses some of the most important do's and don'ts of job hunting, as summarized in Tables 6.1 and 6.2, beginning with the most important. Although many of these points have been mentioned before, this chapter will review some important strategies and tips for the job hunting process.

Do's

Do evaluate your assets brutally, because others will. One of the first do's of job hunting is to look critically at your own record in an attempt to see yourself as others will see you. This is often hard to do for two reasons: First, such a critical examination may hurt if you find areas where you are wanting or where others are better than you are. Criticism, even when self-inflicted, is almost always painful. Yet if you are to go forth

Table 6.1 Do's of Successful Job Searches

- Do evaluate your assets brutally, because others will.
- Do as much as possible to overcome weaknesses in your record.
- Do work with advisers and senior colleagues to help you obtain interviews.
- Do tailor your approach to each employer.
- Do practice your presentation and take it seriously.
- Do realize that your graduate school's reputation will have a bearing on your job search.
- Do remember the importance of attitude and appearance.
- Do realize that previously unappealing job vacancies look more attractive later in the year.
- Do remember that another job search can occur next year, especially if you end up in a temporary or one-year position.

---

into the job market as prepared as you might be to do your best, then a realistic assessment of your strengths and assets is crucial.

What are your strengths? Are you well organized? Personable? Painstaking and methodical? Patient? Engaging and charismatic? Able to convey complex ideas simply? Analytical? Imaginative and creative? Hard working? What about job-related skills? Do you write cogently, concisely, and with power? Do you express yourself well verbally in both formal and informal contexts, or do you rely too heavily upon professional jargon and assume the listener knows too much? Do you have a broad array of professional experience related to your field, such as working with relevant databases, literatures, substances in field or laboratory settings? Can you present a lecture that is well thought out, comprehensive, and well organized? Can you guide discussions skillfully, intervening enough to draw out seminar participants and to keep the conversation on target but not enough to stifle contributions

Table 6.2 Don'ts of Successful Job Searches

- Don't underestimate the competition.
- Don't restrict your search to only safe or sure options.
- Don't forget that universities and colleges have their own interests and peculiarities.
- Don't pretend to be someone you are not.
- Don't act as if you are too good for certain places or tasks; don't put others down.
- Don't appear too eager or desperate.
- Don't lose needed energy near the end.
- Don't expect to find the perfect job the first year.

---

from participants or to dominate the substance of their contributions?

But you must also assess your weaknesses with equal candor: Do you interview well in the sense of presenting an attractive, appealing, and pleasant demeanor, or are you too reticent or bold initially? Do you listen well, or do you have a difficult time letting others speak when you know what they are talking about better than they do? Do you demonstrate an appropriate appreciation for the work of others, or are you interested only in your own work and the research approaches you have studied and used? In terms of research methodologies, are you well versed in a range of them, or do you lack an understanding of those you have not used? Do you write with clarity and ease, or do you struggle with the work, revising and rewriting many times to get an acceptable version? Can you release projects that are good but not perfect, or do you feel compelled to keep polishing a paper and to continue working on it, long past the point of diminishing returns and to the detriment of other projects?

A second difficulty in looking critically at your record from the perspective of future employers, is learning what these employers are looking for. How do you do that? How do you acquire the perspective of those whose experience and years in the profession you do not yet have? If your current PhD department is hiring new professors, attend the interviews. Observe the candidates' presentations, responses to questions and answers, and general demeanor. Afterward, talk with your professors to learn their perspectives of the candidate's strengths and weaknesses. Talking with others who enter the job market before you do may provide another source of information. Finally, scanning job advertisements frequently to see which skills, specializations, and subfields are advertised may alert you to what types of positions colleges and schools are seeking to fill.

Do as much as possible to overcome weaknesses in your record. After critical examination of your own record, what do you do if there are weaknesses or gaps? If you begin the process of self-examination early enough in your graduate school tenure, you might have time to correct some weaknesses. Would adding another subfield specialization make you more attractive to some employers? Is it possible to reword your interests to include specializations that are in ascendancy within your discipline (at least as a teaching option that might appeal to some departments)?

Are you in a discipline where learning the newest statistical and methodological techniques is a way of demonstrating that you are current and up-to-date? If so, investing the time to master one or more new methodologies may be worth it. Brushing up on your computer skills is always a good idea. Computer usage is now important in most if not all fields within academia. Sciences of all types, including physical, biological, and social sciences, have long used computers for database management and statistical analysis. Computers now also permeate the humanities and the arts, as new programs and capacities for analyzing and manipulating documents, texts, and pictures have emerged. Knowing software packages that are relevant to your discipline is surely an advantage when you interview and can be listed as a specific skill on your vita both to demonstrate competency and distinguish yourself from the competition.

Are you in a field where practitioner experience is important, which may be the case in professionally oriented disciplines? If so, internships, research projects, and dissertations that place you in a field of practice should be highlighted in your vita. In other fields, laboratory experience as well as theoretical and classroom training may increase your appeal.

In most disciplines today, having actual teaching experience may make you more appealing. Increasingly, most colleges and many universities are emphasizing teaching. Have information on your past teaching, such as evaluations from courses you have taught, copies of syllabi you have developed, and perhaps even samples of syllabi of courses you would enjoy teaching within your specialization, ready to send to prospective employers along with research papers and samples from your dissertation.

Do work with advisers and senior colleagues to help you obtain interviews. How do you obtain an invitation to interview at a campus that has a job you want? Horror stories abound of graduating PhDs who send out hundreds of vitae and job applications to distant schools without getting a single interview. Your academic advisers and professors are very important in helping you obtain job interviews. Sometimes a timely and helpful phone call from your adviser or a professor on your committee to a colleague on a job search committee at another institution can be invaluable in making sure your name and application bubble up from the morass of applications all the way to the short list. The more respected and well regarded your advisers and committee members are, the better able they will be to help you get serious attention at other universities and colleges with jobs.

Proactive advisers who are always thinking about your future and how to enhance it may do this naturally and without prodding. But many faculty are busy with their own affairs and may not think of placing a crucial call unless you politely prompt them or express concern about a particular job where you know informal contact from your faculty could help. To do this, you must know the backgrounds of the faculty in your graduate department. Where did they obtain their PhDs, study as undergraduates, go on sabbatical? Do they have long-term coauthors, collaborators, or friends at other universities and, if so, which ones? The more you know about the backgrounds of your own professors, the more you may be able to realize when they can help you in your job search.

Do tailor your approach to each employer. Although it can be extra work, think about each job specifically. Most of the tailoring will come in your letter of application to the prospective employer. If a department advertises for one subfield specialization, then your letter of application and accompanying vita should emphasize that coursework and experience ecompassing the required subfield. If you apply for a job in a department where one subfield is stated as the primary concern and your vita and application letter stress a different subfield, your application might be tossed out on the first round.

If you have diversified in graduate school to pick subfields that not only interest you but improve your job prospects, you may now have the flexibility of packaging yourself in several different ways. You might initially write two or three different application letters, each emphasizing a particular aspect of your record. Similarly, you might make an equivalent number of copies of your vita. Again, each different version would highlight different areas of subspecialization. In Version A, the courses you took in Subfield A might be listed first, along with that subfield as one of your primary research and teaching areas. In Version B, list the courses you took in Subfield B first, and state that Subfield B is one of your primary research and teaching areas. You do not want to make inaccurate claims or lie about what you can and will do once you get the job, but shape your application within the constraints of what you have legitimately studied.

Do practice your presentation and take it seriously. Typically, you will be expected to make a presentation to allow the hiring department to see you in action and to demonstrate your research and analytical skills. Some candidates will always be better at organization and delivery than others. But for everyone, even for those gifted at public presentations of complex projects and ideas, it always helps to practice before your friends and colleagues (see Chapter 3). Before you go on the job market, organize and write up your talk, paying careful attention to details, overheads, and other visuals that will enable you to get your points across clearly and succinctly.

Do realize that your graduate school's reputation will have a bearing on your job search. Most departments with a position to fill will look for a job candidate whose background looks similar to that of faculty already employed at the institution. If the faculty were trained at Ivy League and other similarly prestigious schools, most likely they will search for job candidates who were also trained at prestigious universities. Large state universities may vary in their expectations, depending on the backgrounds of the particular faculty and administrators involved. But they will typically look for a candidate with credentials as impressive as their own and possibly better. Rarely do departments favor candidates from universities considered lower in status than their own. Smaller colleges may also vary significantly, but administrators at such colleges often view the credentials of the faculty as one of the most important marketing attributes of the college in recruiting students. The better the faculty in terms of visible criteria, the easier it is to recruit prospective students and to raise funds.

What does this mean for your job search? It does not mean that you should never apply for a job at a university that is rated better in national rankings than the one from which you are receiving your PhD. Rather, it means you should be aware of the importance that many people place on the overall prestige of the institution from which you received your PhD and diversify your applications. Apply to some selected universities that are ranked better, but also apply to some considered at the same level, and to some that are ranked lower, to maximize your chances of obtaining a tenure-track job.

Do remember the importance of attitude and appearance. In job searches, presenting an image of collegiality and pleasantness can go a long way and, in some instances, make up for other flaws such as not having trained at the most prestigious PhD institution. Although your being pleasant will not overcome some weaknesses in your record, everything else being equal, collegiality will provide you with a competitive edge. Faculty members of the hiring department know that they must live with this person for some time and want to find a candidate who not only will meet the department's intellectual needs but who will also be pleasant to work with.

Although we often want to believe that people pay attention to what we say, not how we look, potential colleagues will take your appearance into account in forming an overall judgment. Books on dressing for success have long inundated the business world. The reality is that seemingly trivial matters such as inappropriate or ill-fitting clothing may cause some prospective employers to make judgments about you that you would not like, and your appearance signals certain aspects of your personality that are hard to retract or reverse once they have been transmitted. Few prospective employers would label a male applicant who showed up for an interview in worn blue jeans, hiking boots, a faded jacket, and long hair in a pony tail as "traditional" or "conservative" or even "proinstitutional." Similarly, a Brooks Brothers' suit, an expensive leather briefcase, a short-cropped haircut, and a white shirt would hardly convey antiauthoritarianism or radicalism. Female candidates who show up in short skirts, tight tops, and heavy jewelry will likely evoke a negative response. Those who show up in baggy clothing, love beads, sandals, and unshaved legs may interview well in the most feminist of women's studies programs but not necessarily as well in traditional disciplines.

Some careful attention to what you wear both at professional conventions when you are looking for a job and at campus interviews may pay off in big dividends and surely cannot hurt. Most candidates beginning a job search will go out and purchase two or three outfits that convey an atmosphere of professionalism to wear on such occasions. Obviously your own personality, physique, and the size of your bank account will determine what and how much you purchase. But each item and outfit should be evaluated for the overall impression it conveys. In general, it is wise to avoid extremes and fads. Indulge propensities that deviate toward the extreme after you have landed the job, not before. A traditional interview suit is one that is neatly tailored, fits well, and conservative in color and fabric. Social clothes for dinner should also be conservative and modest. In general, clothing should not draw attention to you—use your ideas, knowledge, and skills to do that.

In the general culture, women have greater latitude selecting professional clothing than do men. But for women on job interviews, erring on the side of being conservative in both hairstyle and dress is preferable to erring toward the flamboyant. The same caveat is also true for racial and ethnic minority candidates. A rule of thumb is that people are allowed one idiosyncratic chit when they interview for a job. In white-male-dominated departments, which are still the norm in academia, women and minorities use up their idiosyncratic chit just by who they are—in that environment, being a woman or member of a minority is itself idiosyncratic. To add in flamboyant or radical clothing is to use two chits, one more than most candidates are allowed before creating subconscious psychological stress.

Do realize that previously unappealing job vacancies will look more attractive later in the year. Early in the season, you may be choosy about what you consider to be an appropriate job, hoping for the job that best suits your needs and career ambitions. But if as the season wears on you have not been invited to interview for the best job, or even been contacted by institutions that are your first priority, then you may find other jobs becoming more appealing simply by default. You may reevaluate your chances and options and become more realistic as the season advances. In some instances, this dynamic may force you to look at jobs you would not have otherwise considered, where you may actually be happier and which you may be better suited to than those you initially preferred. In other instances, you may be prepared to accept jobs you still consider to be second-rate. Whichever is the case, your idea of a realistic job shifts as the job hunting season advances so that by the end you consider options you would not have considered at the beginning.

Do remember that another job search may occur again the following year, especially if you end up in a temporary or one-year position. Suppose your first foray into the job market does not result in a successful match between you and an employer. What do you do? Despair and depression may result, but remembering that another job market will open up next year may help to minimize these natural tendencies. Your inability to get a suitable job on your first job market entry may not prevent you from finding one the following year. Given the tightening job market, many candidates may hold several one-year positions such as sabbatical replacements before being successful at finding a tenure-track job. Sometimes, the PhD granting school may try to keep the job candidate around for another year, perhaps working on a project or a postdoctoral fellowship. In other instances, the job candidate may fill in for someone on sabbatical on an adjunct or part-time basis. During this period, the still-searching job candidate can complete the dissertation, develop articles for publication from the dissertation, perhaps initiate another research project and deliver a conference paper or two, and gain teaching experience. With these additional assets and experience, the candidate then enters the job market the next year, slightly older, wiser, and with experience and accomplishments that may provide a competitive advantage.

Don'ts

Following several rules of thumb of things not to do will enhance your job seeking efforts and increase your prospects of success.

Don't underestimate the competition. One problem with job searching is determining who and what the competition is. Although you may know who the other job candidates are at your own PhD school, most departments do not graduate more than a handful of PhDs in a single year. The other candidates at your own institution may not be in your subfields and may not be looking at the exact same jobs as you are. How, then, do you judge the competition? If you do not have a sense of who the competition is, a natural tendency is to underestimate and downplay the assets and experience of other job candidates.

It is not necessary and is probably impossible to know all the individuals who are competing against you for jobs in your areas of specialization. You can obtain some perspective on their relative strengths and weaknesses by going to both regional and national conventions a year or two before you go onto the job market and, when possible, looking at the formal credentials of those who are using the job finding services of conventions. Informal discussions at conventions with others may also provide some information on this topic. Some conventions organize special graduate student panels and cocktail parties where you may meet prospective job candidates from other institutions.

If your department is conducting a job search for a position at the appropriate level, ask to look at the credentials of candidates applying. In most departments, after a job search committee has narrowed down the prospective number of candidates to a short list, the credentials of those candidates are placed in some central location for examination and comment by other department members who are not on the job search committee. Looking at the credentials of candidates on the short list may give you a sense of what types of training, expertise, teaching experience, research skills, publications, and professional presentations are desirable in those job candidates considered to be competitive by your PhD institution.

Don't restrict your search to only safe or sure options. You do not want to paper the country with applications that are mostly unrealistic, but given your background, training, and experience, it may also be a mistake to limit your job search to only safe or sure options. Lowering your ambitions to only those universities and colleges where you may be considered highly qualified may not guarantee you a job at any one of them, because the market may be flooded with job candidates, or budget cuts may cause many of those sure positions to disappear. You'll also be preventing yourself from shooting high in at least some instances. The trick, then, is to have a few long shots among those schools to which you apply but, at the same time, to try to make sure that you indeed have some probability greater than zero of being considered. When search committees receive applications from candidates they consider inappropriate, they are often quickly tossed into the discard pile. Applying to large numbers of schools where you have little possibility of being seriously considered is a waste of time, energy, and resources and may make you appear shopworn. But not applying to any long shots is equally unwise. For a few candidates, long shots pay off.

Don't forget that universities and colleges have their own interests and peculiarities. Employers have interests of their own, and those interests differ from yours (see Chapter 1). In theory, departments want the best possible candidate, and candidates want the best possible job. Ideally, the market should bring them together in a way that optimizes the interests of both sides. Theory sometimes differs from reality. At times, really exceptional candidates may threaten one or more persons in the job searching department, and job candidates may have personal interests to balance with their professional ones. The interests of those at the employing college or university will reflect a combination of personal and institutional preferences, which may only marginally overlap with your interests. If, however, you can ascertain what those preferences are, through formal and informal means, you are better situated to know how to respond to a prospective employer and, indeed, whether or not to respond at all.

Don't pretend to be someone you are not. Pretension does not lead to genuine, happy relationships in job searches. Although you should try to tailor your application and vita to respond to the needs and requests of the employing institution and department, this does not mean you should bend your image and presentation into something that is not accurate. You should not pretend to be someone you are not, for such pretension will eventually catch up with you. If you pretend to have job skills you do not have and are hired on the basis of those assertions, the department that hires you will likely figure out soon after you are hired that you exaggerated and pretended. Not only will your own credibility be tarnished, but so will the credibility of your graduate school mentors and professors. The reputations you damage may be more than your own. If you pretend to have interests in subfields and teaching areas that you do not have, then you will likely be stuck doing these for some time after you are hired. The best rule of thumb here is to agree only to things that you are really willing to do. Then later you cannot be accused of trying to be someone you are not.

Don't act as if you are too good for certain places or tasks; don't put others down. Graduate students can sometimes act arrogantly. Some students convince themselves that no one else quite has the valuable knowledge they do, particularly on topics over-lapping their dissertation. Furthermore, if you have been at a high-powered PhD granting university in a prestigious department, you may have been accepted by well regarded professors and taken into their confidence. As these professors acknowledge your abilities and begin to mentor you, you may feel that they have accepted you, if not as an equal, at least as a potential equal. After experiencing such a heady and high-powered environment, you may then find yourself being interviewed by professors who are not as prestigious, well regarded, or widely published as your mentors, and you may display a sense of hubris about your standing as compared to theirs. This does not lead to offers.

A related issue is to watch what you say about others. When you are interacting with faculty at a campus interview, some of them may try to draw you into speaking poorly of others, including your mentors and PhD professors, your fellow graduate students, administrators at your PhD university, or others with whom you have had a professional relationship. Even if the person who is pushing you in this direction seems superficially friendly, do not be drawn into such discussions, as you do not know their motives or their relationship to the person or persons they are encouraging you to attack. Nor do you fully understand the position of that person within the hiring institution. Even if the persons listening to you agree with your negative views, they may come to see you as someone who is willing to disparage and put down others, not a job hiring characteristic on the top of most prospective employers' lists.

If you hold negative views of key people in your discipline, especially those at your PhD university, you are better off keeping those views to yourself and making noncommittal replies to any questions that veer off in that direction. In addition, if you are critical of a senior faculty member of high reputation, you may also be seen as naively arrogant. This is not to say that you should not provide well-reasoned critiques of the intellectual works of senior colleagues in your discipline and even in your PhD institution. But reasoned and dispassionate critiques of a senior colleague's work are quite different in temper, tone, and perception from personal attacks. Personal attacks are best avoided generally, especially when you are in the job market.

Don't appear too eager or desperate. Balance your desire for a job with an appropriate level of reserve and enthusiasm. If you appear to be overly compliant or willing to do or say anything, you will be seen as having few or no other possibilities of employment, or even worse, as a candidate no one else wants. Recall that most departments want to hire the best possible candidate that they can, and a candidate that no one else wants hardly fits that description! The line between being pleasant and cordial and flexible, on the one hand, and overly eager and desperate, on the other, may be a fine one, but once you have strayed over it, changing your image and correcting that impression may be quite difficult.

Other than promising to teach any and everything in their college catalog, what makes you appear too eager? Not asking penetrating questions on a job interview may give the impression that you do not care about crucial aspects of the job or are so eager to get the job that you are not discriminating. But the behavior that is most likely to generate a perception of over-eagerness is calling the hiring department often and at inappropriate times before they have made a decision. If you have an offer elsewhere and have to make a decision about whether or not to accept it, calling a department which has interviewed you to inquire about your status is alright, especially if you state why you need this information. Similarly, if a lengthy period of time (six weeks to two months) has transpired with no word forthcoming from a college or university you had visited, calling the chair of the search committee again to inquire about your status would not be inappropriate.

Don't lose needed energy near the end. Almost anyone who engages in serious job hunting will tell you that the process can be exhausting. Scanning job information and then applying, developing job applications, tailoring your vita, writing appropriate cover letters, preparing your talk, and going on interviews can be exhausting. Attending conventions to go through job locator services and conducting short interviews there are also time- and energy-consuming.

If you are called for a campus interview, working out the dates and details sometimes takes more time than the actual visit of two or three days. Interviews themselves can be exhausting, including travel that may or may not go as planned, long days when you are constantly supposed to be on your best behavior and making your best impression, and social occasions, probably including dinner with key faculty and search committee members, during which you will be asked questions about your background and career plans and your responses scrutinized.

This entire process occurs when you may be feverishly working on your dissertation and teaching. As you progress through the job season, you may become tired and just want the process to end. Multiple campus interviews in rapid succession can be particularly wearing. At an interview in which you have been asked the same questions for the umpteenth time, you may have an urge to give in to the fatigue and either answer curtly or appear unresponsive. But remember that the time to show your tiredness is when you are back home, after you have done your best to perform and demonstrate your potential, not while you are still out on an interview visit. Remember, the job you save by postponing fatigue may be your own.

Don't expect to find the perfect job the first year. Perhaps you will be one of the fortunate ones who finds a job on your first foray into the job market. Part of doing so may be a function of planning and careful calculation, but part may be a function of luck or random chance. Whereas many people are fortunate to locate jobs on their first try, many are not, especially in the current academic marketplace. Anticipate that finding an acceptable job will require several interviews and, possibly, several years, with temporary appointments at first. Do not just give up after a year of being unable to find the perfect job.

Conclusions and Lessons

We hope this book's tips about searching for an academic job will be useful to you. This chapter has outlined some of the most important things to remember to do and to refrain from doing as part of the job search process. Review these from time to time to help sharpen your job search approach, especially before attending professional meetings and campus interviews. Be optimistic and appropriately confident. As always, luck never hurts, but luck comes to those who help it along by being prepared for opportunities.

References

Anthony, R., & Roe, G. (1984). *Finding a job in your field; A handbook for PhDs and MAs*. Princeton, NJ: Peterson's Guides.

Heiberger, M. M., & Vick, J. M. (1992). *The academic job search handbook.* Philadelphia: University of Pennsylvania Press.

Lewis, A. (1988). *The best resumes for scientists and engineers.* New York: John Wiley.

Magner, D. K. (1994, April 27). The job market blues. *Chronicle of Higher Education.*

Mahtesian, C. (1995, July). Higher ed: The no longer sacred cow. *Governing*, pp. 20-26.

Ory, J. C., & Ryan, K. E. (1993). *Tips for improving testing and grading.* Newbury Park, CA: Sage.

Rice, R. W. (1986). *Finding a job in higher education in art education.* Reston, VA: National Art Education Association.

Tierney, E. P. (1996). *How to make effective presentations.* Thousand Oaks, CA: Sage.

Weimer, M. (1993). *Improving your classroom teaching.* Newbury Park, CA: Sage.

Whicker, M. L., Kronenfeld, J. J., & Strickland, R. A. (1993). *Getting Tenure.* Newbury Park, CA: Sage.

Additional Resources

For additional information on job searches and career planning, read the following:

Anagnoson, J. T. (1994, September). Netting the big one: Some things candidates (and departments) ought to know . . . from the hiring department's perspective. *PS*, 558-562.

Baumgardner, S. R. (1989). *College and jobs: Conversations with recent graduates.* New York: Human Sciences Press.

Berger, A. A. (1993). *Improving writing skills.* Newbury Park, CA: Sage.

Bess, J. L. (1982). *University organization.* New York: Human Sciences Press.

Beveridge, D., & Davidson, J. P. (1986). *The achievement challenge.* Homewood, IL: Dow Jones-Irwin.

Bolles, R. N. (1991). *What color is your parachute? A practical manual for job-hunters and career-changers.* Berkeley, CA: Ten Speed Press.

Bowen, H. R., & Schuster, J. H. (1986). *American professors: A national resource imperiled.* New York: Oxford University Press.

Bowser, B. P., Auletta, G. S., & Jones, T. (1993). *Confronting diversity issues on campus.* Newbury Park, CA: Sage.

Breneman, D. W., & Youn, T. I. K. (1988). *Academic labor markets and careers.* New York: Falmer.

Burton, M. L., & Wedemeyer, R. A. (1991). *In transition.* New York: Harper-Business.

Clark, B. R. (Ed.). (1987). *The academic profession.* Berkeley: University of California Press.

Finkelstein, M. J. (1984). *The American academic profession.* Columbus: Ohio State University Press.

Fox, J. R., & Levin, J. (1993). *How to work with the media.* Newbury Park, CA: Sage.

Furlong, D. K., & Furlong, S. R. (1994, March). Netting the big one: Things candidates (and departments) ought to know. *PS,* 84-90.

Furniss, W. T. (1981). *Reshaping faculty careers.* Washington, DC: American Council on Education.

Gmelch, W. H. (1993). *Coping with faculty stress.* Newbury Park, CA: Sage.

Henze, G. (1992). *Winning career moves.* Homewood, IL: Business One Irwin.

Kaplan, R. M. (1991). *The whole career sourcebook.* New York: AMACOM.

Metzger, R. O. (1993). *Developing a consulting practice.* Newbury Park, CA: Sage.

Schuster, J. H., Wheeler, D. H., & Associates. (1990). *Enhancing faculty careers.* San Francisco: Jossey-Bass.

Smedley, C. S., Allen, M., & Associates. (1993). *Getting your book published.* Newbury Park, CA: Sage.

Webster, D. S. (1986). *Academic quality rankings of American colleges and universities.* Springfield, IL: Charles C Thomas.

Yost, E. B., & Corbishley, M. A. (1987). *Career counseling: A psychological approach.* San Francisco: Jossey-Bass.

About the Authors

Jennie Jacobs Kronenfeld (PhD, Brown University, 1976) is Professor of Health Administration in the College of Business at Arizona State University in Tempe. She has published 5 books and 100 articles in the areas of health services research, health administration, health education, health policy, and women and health. She also has specialized in survey research on health issues.

Marcia Lynn Whicker (PhD, University of Kentucky, 1976) is Professor of Public Administration at the Graduate School at Rutgers, Newark. Her publications include 12 books, more than 45 peer-reviewed articles, and more than 50 nonpeer-reviewed and journalistic articles in the areas of public policy, public administration, and U.S. politics. Her interests include using computer-simulation models to test the effectiveness and representativeness of governmental structures and systems.